TOP SHOT

Foreword by *Top Shot's* COLBY DONALDSON

Text by DON RAUF

NEW AMERICAN LIBRARY

NEW AMERICAN LIBRARY
Published by New American Library, a division of
Penguin Group (USA) Inc., 375 Hudson Street,
New York, New York 10014, USA
Penguin Group (Canada), 90 Eglinton Avenue East, Suite 700, Toronto,
Ontario M4P 2Y3, Canada (a division of Pearson Penguin Canada Inc.)
Penguin Books Ltd., 80 Strand, London WC2R 0RL, England
Penguin Ireland, 25 St. Stephen's Green, Dublin 2,
Ireland (a division of Penguin Books Ltd.)
Penguin Group (Australia), 250 Camberwell Road, Camberwell, Victoria 3124,
Australia (a division of Pearson Australia Group Pty. Ltd.)
Penguin Books India Pvt. Ltd., 11 Community Centre, Panchsheel Park,
New Delhi - 110 017, India
Penguin Group (NZ), 67 Apollo Drive, Rosedale, Auckland 0632,
New Zealand (a division of Pearson New Zealand Ltd.)
Penguin Books (South Africa) (Pty.) Ltd., 24 Sturdee Avenue,
Rosebank, Johannesburg 2196, South Africa

Penguin Books Ltd., Registered Offices:
80 Strand, London WC2R 0RL, England

First published by New American Library,
a division of Penguin Group (USA) Inc.

First Printing, November 2012
10 9 8 7 6 5 4 3 2 1

 REGISTERED TRADEMARK—MARCA REGISTRADA

LIBRARY OF CONGRESS CATALOGING-IN-PUBLICATION DATA:

Top shot/foreword by Top shot's Colby Donaldson.
p. cm.
ISBN 978-0-451-41345-1
1. Shooting. 2. Sports tournaments. I. Top shot (Television program)
GV1153.T68 2012
799.3'1—dc23   2012013850

Set in Din and Univers LT Std
Designed by Pauline Neuwirth

PUBLISHER'S NOTE
Outdoor recreational activities are by their very nature potentially hazardous. All participants in such
activities must assume the responsibility for their own actions and safety. If you have any health
problems or medical conditions, consult with your physician before undertaking any outdoor activities.
The information contained in this guidebook cannot replace sound judgment and good decision making,
which can help reduce risk exposure; nor does the scope of this book allow for disclosure of all the
potential hazards and risks involved in such activities. Learn as much as possible about the outdoor
recreational activities in which you participate, prepare for the unexpected, and be cautious. The reward
will be a safer and more enjoyable experience.

    While the author has made every effort to provide accurate telephone numbers, Internet addresses,
and other contact information at the time of publication, neither the publisher nor the author assumes
any responsibility for errors, or for changes that occur after publication. Further, publisher does not
have any control over and does not assume any responsibility for author or third-party Web sites or
their content.

CONTENTS

SEASON ONE

SEASON TWO

SEASON THREE

SEASON FOUR

FOREWORD

Colby Donaldson

I LEARNED TO shoot when I was six years old and that experience is one of my best childhood memories. My father taught me on a Winchester single-shot .22 rifle that was the first gun that he bought when he was a kid. When he was twelve years old, he walked down to the local hardware store (back then, you could buy rifles from the hardware store)—and each week he put a dollar down on a layaway. He was mopping floors at a restaurant and he was making a dollar a week. After twenty weeks of hard work mopping floors, he was the proud owner of that rifle. And I was proud to learn how to squeeze the trigger on that same rifle. I've been into guns ever since.

As a gun enthusiast and someone who wants to constantly get better at shooting, I have had the great pleasure of hosting *Top Shot* on the History Channel since season one of the program. In the show, sixteen contestants who have proven themselves to be excellent marksmen compete against one another for the title of Top Shot. Our competition is designed to find the very best marksman—the man or woman who can hit *any* target—from the head of a nail to a cotton swab. And they often have to perform under *extreme* situations, using a range of weapons, including historical flintlock pistols, modern semiautomatic rifles, and ancient tools, such as the tomahawk.

What are some of those extreme situations? Try zooming down a zip line, traversing four hundred feet with a hundred-foot drop, while shooting at marks with a pistol. Or try blasting targets while strapped to what looks like the hand of a giant clock, spinning 360 degrees around, reaching a height of forty feet in the air, where you are completely upside down.

We're the only show on television that uses 100 percent live ammunition. There are no blanks. There are no Hollywood stunt guns. These are all real firearms shooting real bullets.

Often, the weapons we feature have played an important role in history. A lot of people think we're using prop guns or replicas, but these are real period pieces. The tommy guns featured in season two were actual Thompson submachine guns from 1928 and 1929. Competitors have fired the Browning Automatic Rifle (BAR) from World War I, flintlock rifles and pistols that date back to the American Revolution, and even a huge bag gun cannon used during the Spanish-American War.

You can't help being awed when those guns appear on the set. I remember when the Gatling gun showed up—there was no way that I was going to let that thing leave without hand-cranking it and sending some rounds downrange. On my bucket list of cool things that I wanted to do growing up was to shoot a fully automatic machine gun. I had the opportunity to do that on *Top Shot* with the tommy gun and the BAR.

I love the history of the weapons we feature. My grandfather was a bomber pilot in World War II, and my father served in Vietnam, so a lot of the military weapons have interested me. My most prized possession is the M1911 that my grandfather carried with him in World War II. So anytime we feature the 1911, I get fired up with a sense of pride.

While the show is certainly about the firearms and other weapons used throughout history, it is really about the marksmen and what it takes to be a Top Shot. With very few exceptions, the men and women who come on the show subscribe to the mantra that to be the best you have to beat the best. That's the way I was raised as a competitor. Regardless of what it is you're competing in, to truly be the victor, you have to put your skills up against those who are the best. By design, *Top Shot* is structured in such a way that you have a chance to prove yourself. You can't be voted off the island like when I was on *Survivor.* You can be nominated for elimination, but as long as you perform well, you won't go home.

The show is constructed on the premise of "may the best marksman win." And that's why the cream rises to the top each season. Iain Harrison, Chris Reed, Dustin Ellermann, and Chris Cheng all proved

themselves to be the best of the best. What did these winners have in common? There's no question, it has to do with attitude. A common denominator with all of our winners was that they were having the most fun throughout the competition. The message is: Love what you do. The winners have had an unwavering focus and the ability to perform under extreme pressure.

Season three winner Dustin Ellermann was the best example of that. He had a blast the entire time. He was not even in the top ten in terms of years of experience or breadth of weapons in his background, but that kid was smiling every time he showed up to a practice session or a challenge. He was having fun and it translated.

Like many of the top performers, Dustin was adaptable. What is unique about *Top Shot* is you have guys who have such extensive backgrounds with weapons. They may be members of the armed forces, law enforcement officers, recreational shooters, or pro shooters like J. J. Racaza. They may be accustomed to speed shooting and hitting difficult targets on a normal gun range, but we're going to put them in an environment that is completely foreign to them.

In season two, we lowered shooters in a prone position from an eighty-foot-high crane. George Reinas was one of those guys with the big bravado and ego coming in, but he didn't want to admit to the fact that he had a huge fear of heights, which he had to overcome.

The challenges pose a kind of pressure different from what any of these guys have ever faced. Obviously, guys with a military background have had bullets whizzing over their heads, so they're going to argue that this is nothing. But there is a different kind of pressure having one hundred crew members standing around and a bunch of cameras recording, and all your buddies and family back home are going to see this.

Sometimes the strongest competitors are unexpected. Like Dustin, Gabby Franco in season four was like that, and she was one of the highlights. It was so refreshing to see a female step up and really deliver. At one point, I asked the guys who they thought their biggest threat was and they all said it was Gabby. It's a credit to her ability as a shooter to adapt to all the different weapons, to remain calm, and perform under pressure. She did it week in and week out. It was a great moment for the series, and I hope more women are getting interested in the show because of her.

The viewers may not realize it, but the weather can pose an additional obstacle for the marksmen. The set is about an hour and fifteen minutes north of Los Angeles, and the weather can be erratic. In the season three sniper challenge with the moving target, the wind was blowing sixty miles per hour. The bullet is going to be affected by crosswinds like that.

There are no weekends off. No days off. It's thirty-six consecutive days of filming. The show must (and always does) go on through wind, fog, rain, sleet, and snow. And while the crew alternates six days of staggered shifts to give them a break and reduce overtime, the competitors and I are on camera every day because of a challenge or practice or nomination range. The competitors stay in a house directly across the road from the ranch where we film, so getting them to set is never a problem. I live in Los Angeles, fifty miles south of the ranch, and it usually takes me an hour to commute early in the morning. In four seasons of filming *Top Shot*, I am proud to say I have never been late to set. Well, except once.

Just before dawn one wet Saturday morning after a heavy rain all night, I pulled out of my driveway only to find the street was blocked by a huge sycamore that had fallen during the storm. I mean this thing was gigantic. It had to have been close to one hundred years old. It was completely barricading the only way in or out of my neighborhood. And because it was a weekend and no one was headed into work early, I was the first one on the scene. Normally, it wouldn't have been that big of a deal. But today, we were scheduled to shoot a lengthy challenge before lunch and at the nomination range in the afternoon. These are the "heavy" days and any holdups or delays completely affect the entire production schedule. You don't want to be the person who forces a hundred-man crew to stand around while the clock is ticking.

After a call to the police, who informed me they would send the fire department out to cut the tree up, I realized I had to come up with an alternate plan.

It would take too long for production to send an intern down to pick me up and I couldn't bum a ride off one of my neighbors since they were in the same predicament I was. So I turned around and parked my truck back at the house. Then I called a cab and told him to start heading up the road to my place. I ran back down, climbed over the tree and kept cruising until I intercepted the cab. We ran a few yellow

lights but ended up making it to the ranch and only delayed the challenge by a half hour or so. End result: I got to keep my job.

Beyond dealing with the whims of the weather, another factor to succeed on *Top Shot* is that you have to be a good individual marksman *as well as* a team player. It's ironic that ultimately succeeding as an individual on *Top Shot* requires that you figure out a way to succeed as a team first. You have to get the green jersey, which is the individual competition stage. The only way you're going to do that is if your red or blue team performs well. So teamwork is a huge part of it. You have to figure out a way to shoot and communicate as a team, not only as an individual. The teams that figure that out more quickly tend to do well. Still, no matter how "kumbaya" your team is, you have got to be able to hit your targets. I think winning is a combination of the two.

Marksmen also have to be adaptable with the weapons. When they come here, they pick up weapons that they never had experience with—especially when they get into primitive weapons like the atlatl or blowgun. One of the most memorable challenges was with the tomahawk in season two. Most competitors had little if any experience with the tomahawk. I don't think any of them thought going in that it would wind up being the most fun that season. It worked out to be one of the closest challenges. It took a lot of strategy to play a type of Connect 4. Not only were you concerned with the skill required to throw your tomahawk, but it took teamwork to figure out the strategy for which square to land that tomahawk in. It ended up being a blast to watch and call live on location. It was a challenge where the weapon itself didn't seem to excite the players that much, but once they go into it, they really wound up enjoying it.

The show is also popular with viewers because of the camera work and how we film the firing of the weapons. I'm continually impressed every time I see a new angle or a new shot. It's a credit to the camera guys. It is a challenge to figure out a new way to cover a shot. I remember breaking for lunch one time, and one of our slow-motion camera crew came back to the mess hall. He was so excited because they had captured a bullet as it had left the muzzle and it broke the sound barrier. You could actually see the bullet pushing the sound waves away from it as it moved. It was a perfect storm—the camera was set in the right position to record that bullet leaving the muzzle, and the lighting was correct.

If you want to become a Top Shot, I think you should invest in a good .22. And I don't think enough guys do that because of ego. But the fundamentals of shooting are the same whether you're squeezing off rounds with a Ruger 10/22 or a Barrett M107 .50-caliber semiautomatic sniper rifle. If you can't hit a target at fifteen to twenty yards with a .22, you're sure not going to hit a four-hundred-yard one with a .338 Lapua rifle. Plus, the ammo is cheaper with your basic .22. Practicing is key. Practice breathing, squeezing the trigger, getting a good site picture, and zeroing the rifle or handgun. Trigger control is essential to becoming a better marksman and there are ways to practice that without buying ammo. You can dry-fire a pistol. When you're sitting around the house, pick up your handgun and just dry-fire it. Get accustomed to the squeeze and break of the trigger. Get used to firing it without actually firing it. You can also practice your reload and your magazine change without having to put live ammo in it and go to the range.

I've learned a lot about becoming a better marksman from the show, and one of the great rewards of hosting is seeing the marksmen evolve during the process—as shooters, as competitors, and even as human beings. Regardless of his or her background or experience, everybody leaves *Top Shot* a better marksman than when he or she arrived. It takes being open to new things, being receptive, maintaining your skills, staying calm, and just having fun.

TOP SHOT™

PISTOLS
AND
HANDGUNS

ALL CULTURES VALUE marksmanship. They wouldn't be here if they didn't. And many people know a bit about using firearms—but *Top Shot* brings together the best of the best to compete for money and glory with historical and cutting-edge weapons in age-old and newly minted contests. The program has featured pistols from as far back as the 1873 Colt Peacemaker—a standard firearm of the Wild West—to the tricked-out, twenty-first-century, Colt-styled Razorcat, used for speed competitions and mounted with a red-dot scope. Season three showed viewers one of the most high-tech examples of firearms, when competitors in the elimination round had to use a 9mm Glock 18 pistol fitted with a "CornerShot." Designed in the early 2000s, the CornerShot attachment lets shooters see—and shoot—around corners.

The earliest pistols date back to the 1380s. These little "hand cannons" have been found in Western Europe and in China. These were single-shot weapons with a very basic operation. The user loaded some gunpowder and a projectile into the muzzle, then ignited it by putting fire to a cord feeding a touchhole. In time, gun makers came up with trigger mechanisms (using a system similar to today's cigarette lighters), and in the seventeenth century, gunsmiths created the flintlock, striking flint against steel to fire ammunition. By the nineteenth century, the revolver came blazing onto the scene, with its innovative cylinder with multiple chambers for ammunition. By the late 1800s the handgun took a leap forward with the invention of the semiautomatic, which uses the energy of one shot to reload the chamber for the next. After firing a round, the gun's recoil energy ejects a spent casing and then chambers a new round from a magazine, making the gun automatically ready to refire. Throughout history, the handgun has played a role in warfare; and law enforcement agents, from sheriffs to today's police officers, have carried them holstered. Handguns have maintained a place in home defense, and been used in many different types of shooting competitions.

Pistols and handguns can be challenging firearms to shoot with great accuracy compared to rifles. Sights can make rifles easier to aim, and the ability to brace the rifle against the shoulder makes them easier to control. Pistols also have limited range. Pistol shooters have to develop proper stance, steady arm control, and strength, along with hand grasp, trigger control, aiming skills, and proper breathing.

"One of the biggest aspects of the shooting sports that a lot of competitors really don't understand is their breathing," says handgun expert Matt Burkett. "And in pistol shooting it's different than in rifle shooting. In rifle shooting you want to fire during the respiratory pause. In pistol shooting a lot of people will hold their breath when they go to shoot. With a pistol that's not a good idea, because once you hold your breath your eyes start to water up and you start losing your vision and it makes it really hard. And the more difficult or awkward the shooting position you're in, the more important breathing is. We might see a big difference in some of the shooters today, but we're helping them just by getting them to continuously and smoothly breathe."

In *Top Shot*, season one, Navy SEAL instructor Craig Sawyer introduces elimination competitors to the TZ 99, a 9mm semiautomatic South African pistol. For James Sinclair, a self-taught shooter who specializes in high-powered rifles, this handgun leads to his elimination against Iain Harrison as they both have to hit targets swinging on a pendulum. "Handguns are not my forte," says Jim.

Pistols vary with trigger control as well. In a season two elimination, competitors Jermaine Finks and Jay Lim face off using a Glock 17, the most prevalent law enforcement sidearm. In practice, Jay has some trouble jerking the trigger, which can disturb the alignment of the pistol. "Jay also started off with an older grip that you don't see," says Sawyer. "I haven't seen it in about thirty years. I advised him as to what the current techniques are and why."

Accuracy with pistols and handguns depends on strong arm and body control. When Gary Quesenberry winds up in the final three, he tries to eliminate Mike Hughes and Dustin Ellermann by having them shoot with just their weak arm. But this strategy proves to be his downfall.

Although common on the firing range on *Top Shot*, handguns have continued to challenge marksmen in feats of accuracy and speed.

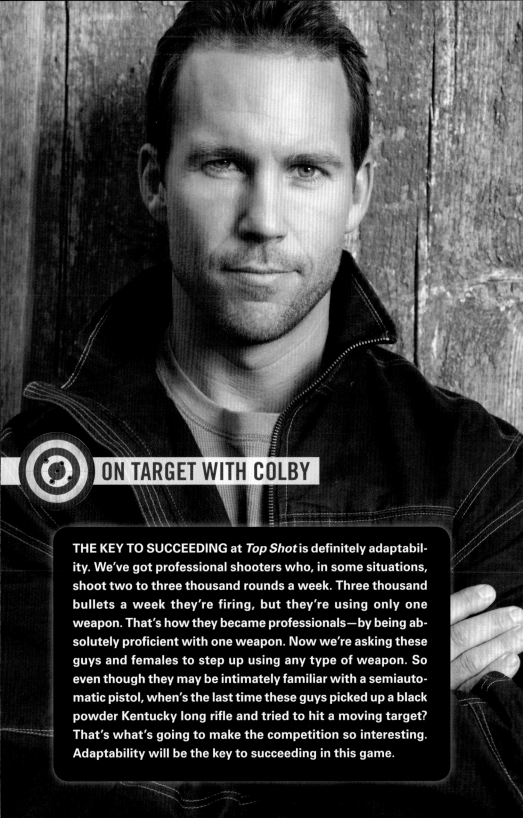

ON TARGET WITH COLBY

THE KEY TO SUCCEEDING at *Top Shot* is definitely adaptability. We've got professional shooters who, in some situations, shoot two to three thousand rounds a week. Three thousand bullets a week they're firing, but they're using only one weapon. That's how they became professionals—by being absolutely proficient with one weapon. Now we're asking these guys and females to step up using any type of weapon. So even though they may be intimately familiar with a semiautomatic pistol, when's the last time these guys picked up a black powder Kentucky long rifle and tried to hit a moving target? That's what's going to make the competition so interesting. Adaptability will be the key to succeeding in this game.

Colt Revolver and Westward Expansion

Samuel **Colt** developed the first revolver in 1836. Suppos-edly Colt was inspired by his sea travels as a young man. He noticed that the helmsman's wheel had a particular clutch and locking, and thought that a similar design could be applied to creating a repeating pistol. He called the gun a revolver, after its patented revolving cylinder, which contained five or six bullets. (That's where the name "six-shooter" comes from.) In the early 1840s, the Colt was first introduced, but it was not a hit—the country was at peace and people saw little need for a rapid-fire weapon. The company went bankrupt in 1842, but Colt's fortune changed in 1846 during the Mexican-American War. The lone survivor of an early battle in the war claimed the Colt had saved his life, and the army ordered a thousand revolvers. By 1855, Colt was the largest arms manufacturer in the world. Samuel

Colt did not live to see it, but the weapon was widely used during the Civil War, and sales skyrocketed.

The Colt Peacemaker of 1873 also became known as "the Gun that Won the West," a standard firearm used throughout the Wild West during the end of the nineteenth century. The classic single-action revolver sold for about $17 at the time. Sheriffs relied on the Colt, as did hustlers and desperadoes.

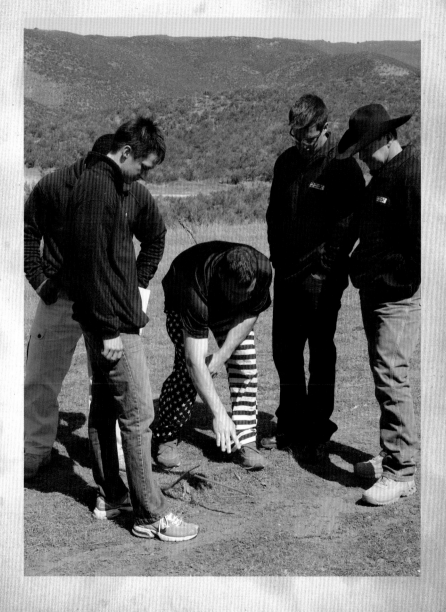

COLT SINGLE-ACTION ARMY REVOLVER
(THE "PEACEMAKER" OR SAA)

COUNTRY: USA

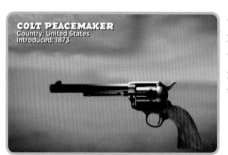

COLT PEACEMAKER
Country: United States
Introduced: 1873

CALIBER: .45

BARREL LENGTH: 7.5 inches

WEIGHT: 2.3 pounds

FEED SYSTEM: Six-round cylinder

COMPETITORS IN SEASON one took on the Colt in a shooting gallery team challenge styled after an Old West storefront. In the elimination round, Kelly Bachand and Andre Robinson played each other in a game of "poker," using the Peacemaker to shoot their cards. One of the most popular firearms in history, this revolver was built by Colt in 1873. This classic American firearm is often associated with the Wild West, and was used by lawmen, frontiersmen, and outlaws. This essential survival tool was for personal safety as well as for hunting. People even used it as a hammer. Over the years Colt has manufactured variations under the names Frontier Six-shooter, Bisley, Target, Flat-top Target, New Frontier, and Buntline.

It shoots a self-contained cartridge, making it a first of its kind, and much easier to load than a muzzle loader. The Peacemaker must be manually cycled between shots, and must be manually unloaded and reloaded by spinning the chamber to load and unload rounds. Standard grips were walnut or black hard rubber.

Dominant Eye

TO AIM, SHOOTERS close one eye and take aim using their dominant eye. The dominant eye is your stronger eye. Most right-handers are right-eye dominant, and most left-handers are left-eye dominant. The International Hunter Education Association suggests this as one method for determining your dominant eye: Point your finger at a distant object with both eyes open. First close one eye and then the other. Your finger should remain lined up with the object when your dominant eye is open. This is just one of many methods to determine your dominant eye.

BERETTA 92F
COUNTRY: ITALY

CALIBER: 9mm

LENGTH: 8.5 inches

WEIGHT: 2.5 pounds loaded/2 pounds unloaded

MAGAZINE CAPACITY: 15 rounds

THIS SEMIAUTOMATIC PISTOL was first designed in 1972 by Beretta, the world's oldest firearms company, for the Italian police force and army. Beretta has been manufacturing firearms for more than five hundred years. The Beretta became the iconic handgun of the 1980s, popularized in movies such as *Die Hard* and *Lethal Weapon*. The pistol is commonly used in law enforcement and is the standard sidearm for the U.S. military.

Open-slide design allows for easy loading and unloading of ammunition. These aluminum-frame, double-action weapons are short-recoil operated and locked-breech.

SMITH & WESSON DOUBLE-ACTION PISTOL
COUNTRY: USA

CALIBER: .38 and .32

BARREL LENGTH: 3¼, 4, 5, and 6 inches

WEIGHT: First .38—1.125 pounds

FEED SYSTEM: 5-round cylinder

CREATED BY THE largest manufacturer of handguns in the United States (based in Springfield, Massachusetts), this pistol can be cocked and fired by a single pull of the trigger (the double action is the cocking and the firing). Smith & Wesson first designed a double-action in 1872.

This handgun has a molded, black, hard-rubber stock. Safety-hammerless versions of these guns are considered to be among the most influential guns S&W ever produced. These were the first revolvers to have hammers completely enclosed within the frame. A shooter could fire only with a long pull on the trigger (termed "double-action only"). A special "hesitation" was built into the trigger pull to allow the user to shoot more precisely, and a grip safety was featured in the back strap (the metal part between the two grips). This required a firm grip on the butt to depress an internal hammer block before the trigger would work.

The story is that D. B. Wesson was concerned when he heard that a child had injured himself by cocking the hammer and pulling the trigger on a standard revolver. So he worked to design a safety mechanism that would require an adult grip to pull the trigger.

GUN TALK

Single-action

Single-action guns need to be cycled by the shooter between shots. After every shot with a single-action revolver, for example, the hammer must be cocked, which makes the revolver ready to fire. With a double-action, semiautomatic, or automatic, all you have to do is pull the trigger.

SCHOFIELD REVOLVER

COUNTRY: USA

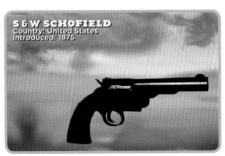

S & W SCHOFIELD
Country: United States
Introduced: 1875

CALIBER: .45

BARREL LENGTH: 7 inches

WEIGHT: 37.9 ounces

FEED SYSTEM: 6-round cylinder

MANUFACTURED FROM 1875 to 1878, this .45 caliber is named after Major George W. Schofield of the 10th Cavalry, who decided to make a refined version of the Smith & Wesson "Model No. 3" to meet his needs in the military. Most were sold to the U.S. military, replacing the Colt Peacemaker.

One of General Schofield's redesigns was to mount the spring-loaded barrel catch on the frame as opposed to the barrel, as with the standard Model 3. With the earlier design, the frame would wear out after heavy use. Schofield also required heat-treated, replaceable components in the areas of the catch and latch, making them more durable.

The army relied on these pistols in the Indian Wars, with some use in the Spanish-American War and the Philippine Insurrection. The gun was popular in the Old West and carried by Buffalo Bill Cody, Frank and Jesse James, John Wesley Hardin, Pat Garrett, Virgil Earp, and Marshal Dallas Stoudenmire.

This is a "top-break" revolver, which is hinged at the bottom front of the cylinder to load the pistol (as opposed to a swing-out cylinder). It also has an automatic ejector. A thumb latch allows the shooter to easily open the gun for loading and unloading with just one hand, and, with practice, to do it all in less than thirty seconds. This was a distinct advantage over the 1873 Colt Peacemaker. The pistol had a standard blue finish and wood grips. (It was the one revolver in the *Top Shot* arsenal that J. J. Racaza knew when he came to the show.)

TZ 99 SOUTH AFRICAN PISTOL

COUNTRY: SOUTH AFRICA

CALIBER: 9x19mm

BARREL LENGTH: 4.25 inches

WEIGHT: 40.2 ounces loaded

FEED SYSTEM: 15-round detachable box magazine

THE ORIGINAL PISTOL was manufactured in the late 1980s at the Crvena Zastava factory located in Kragujevac, Yugoslavia. Reportedly, less than a thousand were imported to the United States. The style of gun was very popular, and many manufacturers made knockoffs. Israel produced a copy called the "Golan."

In the early 1990s, Crvena Zastava came to an agreement with a South African company called Tressitu to manufacture a licensed copy of the CZ 99 called the TZ 99. The company went out of business in the mid-1990s.

The pistol is double-action, recoil operated, with a slide and barrel that lock together through an enlarged chamber area fitting into the ejection port. The slide is made from a single piece of forged and milled steel, and there is a loaded-chamber indicator. Although the TZ 99 has no safety, a decocking mechanism lets the hammer safely lower on a loaded chamber.

SMITH & WESSON M&P REVOLVER
COUNTRY: USA

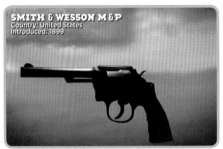

CALIBER: .40

WEIGHT: (Loaded) 35.1 ounces

BARREL LENGTH: The full-size is 4.25 inches

FEEDING SYSTEM: 15-round magazine

THIS SMITH & Wesson semiautomatic military and police revolver is considered one of the most popular revolver designs ever, and is one of the most widely used police revolvers. The first M&P came out in 1899.

Originally these double-action pistols came with swing-out cylinders. The modern M&P is striker-fired, double-action, and magazine-loaded. It has a polymer frame and features a short recoil. It is a locked-breech pistol where the barrel is initially locked to the slide, but the slide is not locked to the grip frame. Improved trigger weight and feel, and a unique takedown method (not requiring a dry pull of the trigger), were meant to set the M&P apart from similar handguns.

.44 MAGNUM
(SMITH & WESSON MODEL 29)
COUNTRY: USA

CALIBER: .44

WEIGHT: 53.5 ounces

BARREL LENGTH: 7.5 inches, but barrel lengths vary between 3 inches and $10\frac{5}{8}$ inches

FEEDING SYSTEM: 6-round cylinder

IN 1955, SMITH & Wesson introduced the legendary .44 Magnum (Model 29), made famous by Clint Eastwood in the Dirty Harry movies in the early 1970s. Travis Bickle (Robert De Niro) also buys one in the movie *Taxi Driver*. It is considered one of the most accurate handguns. Initially designed as a backup weapon for hunters who might go big-game hunting, it can bring down a bear, elk, or bison. The Model 60 is the world's first stainless-steel revolver. The .44 Magnum gets its

name from the type of round it uses—a large-bore cartridge measuring .429 inches in diameter (.44 was just a catchier name and close enough).

The .44 double-action pistol delivers a large bullet at a high velocity. It has a strong recoil, which makes it harder to shoot than some other pistols. Because of the strong recoil and muzzle blast, it is generally considered unsuitable as a police weapon. It has a significant dropout trajectory in ranges of more than a hundred yards. It shoots from a revolving chamber and has a three-dot adjustable rear sight.

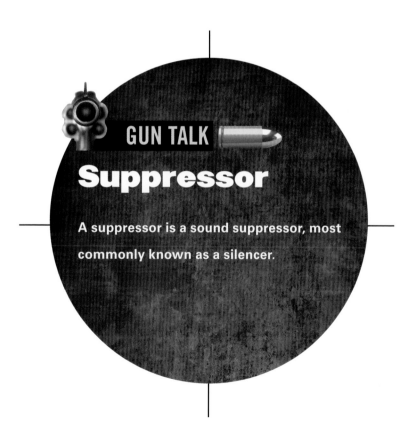

GUN TALK

Suppressor

A suppressor is a sound suppressor, most commonly known as a silencer.

COLT .38 OFFICIAL POLICE REVOLVER
COUNTRY: USA

CALIBER: .38

WEIGHT: 26 ounces, depending on barrel length

BARREL LENGTH: 4-, 5-, and 6-inch models

INTRODUCED IN 1927, the double-action Colt .38 Official Police revolver was hugely popular with police departments. By 1933 departments in Chicago, New York, Kansas City, San Francisco, St. Louis, Portland, and Los Angeles were all using it. State police in Connecticut, Delaware, Maryland, Pennsylvania, and New Jersey also carried the weapon. The FBI also used the gun, and the U.S. government purchased it for security personnel in World War II. Gangsters liked the gun just as much as law enforcement—Al Capone owned a nickel-plated Colt .38 Police Positive, an updated version of the Official Police revolver. Capone's gun has a four-inch barrel and walnut grips. For a relatively heavy gun, the revolver is easy to keep on target, and recoil is not a problem. Colt was in constant competition with Smith & Wesson, and a major selling point of this pistol was that the Colt cylinder turned to the right rather than to the left, as with Smith & Wesson revolvers of the day. Charles Bronson uses a Police Positive with pearl grips in the movie *Death Wish*.

Updating its Army Special revolver, Colt created the Official Police revolver with a wider rear sight groove; rounded, checkered cylinder latch; checkered trigger; and a higher-quality finish—bright royal, Colt blued, and nickel-plated finishes. The sights are a blade front and a V-notch rear. The gun was primarily chambered for the .38 Special cartridge. The Official Police's cylinder swung out by first pulling the cylinder latch to the rear. Pushing in on the ejector rod simultaneously extracted all six spent cases. The Colt Police Positive (the updated version of the Official Police revolver) was named for its "Positive Lock" firing pin block safety, which kept the firing pin from hitting the primer until the trigger was deliberately pulled.

Colt's Second Century and the .38 Official Police Revolver

In 1927, Colt revamped its New Army revolver and renamed it the Colt .38 Official Police revolver, designed to fire the .38 Special cartridge. (Many revolvers that shoot the .38 cartridge are called ".38 Specials.") Often this Colt and other .38 Specials, like the snub-nosed .38, are associated with Prohibition, a nationwide ban on the sale, manufacture, and transportation of alcohol that lasted from 1920 until 1933. The ban was mandated by the Eighteenth Amendment to the Constitution. While Prohibition at first led to a reduction in the amount of alcohol consumed, it also spurred a huge underground organized-crime business centered on producing and selling alcohol illegally. The most famous gangster associated with this activity was Chicago's Al Capone, who became known as "Public Enemy Number One." Capone earned $60 million a year in illegal alcohol sales. He carried a nickel-plated Colt .38 Police Positive, an updated version of the Official Police revolver. "You can get much further with a kind word and a gun than you can with a kind word alone," said Capone. With the Colt .38 and other weapons being used by gangsters and law enforcement alike, violence escalated. Much of America became disenchanted with Prohibition after the St. Valentine's Day Massacre on February 14, 1929, when seven mob members were executed. It is believed that Capone devised the plan to eliminate George "Bugs" Moran due to the rivalry between the two gangs. Prohibition was repealed by the Twenty-first Amendment in 1933.

GUN TALK

Bolt

The bolt is a sliding metal bar that positions the cartridge in breech-loading rifles, closes the breech, and ejects the spent cartridge. Bolt action is one of the simplest types of action on a rifle and tends to result in reliability and accuracy.

"Mission Impossible" Challenge:
SEASON TWO

THE SETUP: With the stakes determining the final four of the season, five finalists face off using the Glock 17. When this semi-automatic 9mm pistol came on the market, it was the world's first polymer-frame handgun. Armed forces and law enforcement agencies around the globe still use it today. For the Glock 17 contest, each player is strapped into a harness and hauled up 125 feet by a construction crane. While in a controlled fall, he or she shoots at ten ground targets placed twenty-five to fifty feet downrange. The shooter who gets the highest number wins.

One at a time, players are strapped into a harness in a prone position and taken to the top of that crane by a cable. On Colby's "Go," they are released in a controlled descent, looking like Tom Cruise in *Mission: Impossible*. As each player plummets straight

down at about twelve feet per second, he or she has to use the Glock 17 to shoot at ten targets that are placed downrange. From 125 feet up, the balloon targets look like marbles. To add to the mix, shooting conditions are rainy, cold, and windy.

THE OUTCOME: During training with the Glock 17, Matt Burkett ran contestants through training that would mimic elements of the elimination, such as having them lie prone on a planklike contraption. The key point Burkett emphasizes is breathing. When players were advised not to hold their breath, they shot much better in the practice sessions. While most players are excited by the challenge, George Reinas appears to be showing some nerves: "I'm not cool being lifted in the air on some rickety contraption on a crane." Brian Zins was excited to take on this competition: "These challenges are designed to take you out of your comfort zone, and that certainly was what this one did today." Jamie Franks, Chris Reed, and Joe Serafini hit four targets, and Brian Zins hits just three. In the end, George, who is most nervous about the competition, walks away with the highest score, hitting six targets, and he earns immunity from elimination. "I don't know if my butt cheeks were shaking so bad because it was cold or because I was nervous going up," George says.

THE ELIMINATION: The final five have to pick who is going to elimination. Jamie is selected and he votes for Chris, sending them both to elimination. Players think that the elimination might again be a pistol competition, but instead the two walk into a practice session firing the Benelli M2 shotgun.

THE ELIMINATION CHALLENGE: Firing from a stationary position with a shotgun might be expected, but Chris and Jamie are loaded in the back of a Humvee and driven at twenty-five miles per hour while shooting at eight clay targets launched in pairs and singles along the route. In the end, Chris takes out five targets and Jamie blasts only three, sending Chris Reed to the final four.

GLOCK 17, 18, 19, AND 34

COUNTRY: AUSTRIA

GLOCK 17
Country: Austria
Introduced: 1982

CALIBER: 9mm Parabellum for all firearms

WEIGHT: (Loaded) 31.91 ounces (17) and 29.98 ounces (19); 23 ounces for the 18, and 32.79 ounces for the 34

BARREL LENGTH: 4.5 inches (17), 4.5 inches (18), 4 inches (19), 5.32 inches (34)

FEEDING SYSTEM: 17-cartridge standard magazine (17), 33-round magazine (18), 15-cartridge standard (19), 17-cartridge standard (34)

GLOCKS HAVE BEEN used throughout the *Top Shot* series. Sometimes called the Glock "Safe-Action" pistol, this semiautomatic was invented by Gaston Glock, an engineer with no background in firearms or manufacturing. He did, however, have a deep knowledge of advanced synthetic polymers, and when the Austrian army put out the call for a new, modern-duty pistol to replace their old World War II handguns, Glock assembled a team of handgun experts and developed a prototype. When it was introduced, there was resistance to accepting a "plastic" gun. Today, the Glock is the most widely used law enforcement pistol worldwide. Although the Glock 17 has a magazine capacity of seventeen, it is actually named because that version is the seventeenth patent on the weapon.

This firearm is known for its above-average magazine capacity of seventeen, light weight, and reliability. Glocks are made with three independent safety mechanisms to prevent accidental discharge. The Glock is known for its ergonomic design that makes it comfortable to hold for both right-handed or left-handed users. Tenifer surface treatment protects its solid, cold-hammered barrels and slides, giving them an extra-hard surface. The Glock 19 is smaller, lighter, more compact, and has a smaller standard magazine capacity. The grip of the 19 is also shorter than the 17, and the guns have a different overall feel. The longer barrel of the 17 gives a longer sight radius.

More distance between front and rear sights allows for more pre-cise alignment, but wobble may increase. (One pistol shooter who has used four-, five-, and 7.5-inch barrels found that he shot best with the five-inch—the four-inch was less exacting for aim because of the short sight radius; the longer was less accurate because of sight wobble and barrel drop.) The Glock 18 machine pistol has the same features as the 17, but in a selective-fire format—automatic and semiautomatic. The Glock 34 has an extended barrel length for high accuracy and is used often in international pistol shooting com-petitions.

GLOCK 34
COUNTRY: AUSTRIA
INTRODUCED: 1998

Glock 17—Matt Burkett
(Director of Predator Tactical)

I'VE BEEN A professional shooter for over twenty years and teaching all the different aspects of competition. The Glock 17 is a unique gun in that it's the world's first polymer pistol. Over two and a half million units of this gun have been produced world wide, and the 9mm is in use by military and law enforcement agencies all over. The seventeen-round magazine on a Glock makes it easy to carry three times as much ammo as a revolver. The trigger control on the Glock 17 is one of the critical things to shooting that gun well. To shoot it accurately, you have to actually pull it differently from a lot of the other guns in the marketplace. And so one of the things we work on is called "pinning the trigger." With a Glock, that's holding the trigger to the rear for at least a quarter of a second while the gun recoils and then feeling the reset, which is a loud click.

There are different ways of aiming a handgun, and these have advantages, depending on the target difficulty. If you've got a really large, up-close target you can pretty much use a total-body index. You just put the image of the gun inside of the target. If it all fits inside of the target, there's a real high percentage or probability of hitting that target. You can also use a flash sight picture, which means you've actually established that you can clearly see the sights on top of the handgun. From a flash sight picture you go to a confirmed and aligned sight picture, which means your sights are actually lined up on the target. The most accurate type of aiming is the confirmed sight picture with a recoil lift. So you actually see the front sight lift as the firearm goes off. That's the most accurate type of shooting, but a lot of the time in the competition stuff you don't necessarily have time to be able to get the sight picture with the recoil lift.

SIX-ROUND CYLINDER COLT .45 1911

COUNTRY: USA

CALIBER: .45 cartridge

WEIGHT: (government model) 2 pounds, 7 ounces

BARREL LENGTH: (government model) 5 inches

FIRING SYSTEM: 7-round standard magazine with 1 in the chamber

DEVELOPED IN 1911 by John Browning and chambered for the .45 ACP cartridge, the Colt .45 1911 is a single-action, semiautomatic, maga-zine-fed, recoil-operated handgun. The gun was adopted by the U.S. Army on March 29, 1911, giving it the name M1911. From 1911 to 1985, this was the standard-issue sidearm for the U.S. armed forces and widely used in World War I, World War II, the Korean War, and the Vietnam War.

Browning was known for perfecting the short-recoil operation. Basically, expanding combustion gases force the bullet down the barrel, giving reverse momentum to the slide and barrel, which are locked together during this portion of the firing cycle. After the bul-let has left the barrel, the slide and barrel move rearward a short distance. When the barrel slides rearward, a claw extractor pulls the spent casing from the firing chamber and sends it out and away from the pistol. As the slide then moves forward, propelled by a spring, it picks up a fresh cartridge from the magazine and feeds it into the fir-ing chamber. The system allows a user to shoot repeatedly by simply pulling the trigger.

2X RAZORCAT
(MODIFIED 2011)
COUNTRY: USA

CALIBER: 9mm Super or .38 Super

BARREL LENGTH: With compensator, 6.5 inches (short); 7 inches (long)

FEEDING SYSTEM: 20-round magazine

NAMED AFTER *TOP Shot* season one contestant J. J. Racaza and manufactured by Limcat, this gun is a "Colt .45 1911 on steroids," says Racaza. With fewer than a hundred of these pistols in existence, the limited edition 2011 Razorcat is a custom-made, tricked-out version of the Colt built for speed competitions. The pistol is designed for open division USPSA (United States Practical Shooting Association) and IPSC (International Practical Shooting Confederation) competition.

The difference between this gun and the Colt is that instead of front and rear sights, a red-dot scope allows the shooter to put a red dot on the target, and that's where the bullet should hit. Shooters have to be aware that the scope dot is an inch and a half above the barrel. It has about a two-pound trigger pull, compared to many pistols that have a six-pound trigger pull. It is the definition of "hair trigger." A compensator reduces recoil. It has a thicker grip than the traditional Colt because of the high capacity. Velocity compares to that of an assault rifle. The gun costs $4,500. It features the new long-threaded V-6 Razorcomp and L-Cut slide. It can be chambered for 9mm Super or .38 Super cartridges. The 9mm Supers are loaded to higher pressures. Bullet velocities and energy levels are much greater than typical factory-loaded ammunition for those calibers.

RUGER SECURITY SIX .357 MAGNUM

COUNTRY: USA

CALIBER: .357

WEIGHT: 4-inch barrel—33.5 ounces

BARREL LENGTH: 2.75 inches, 4 inches, and 6 inches

FEEDING SYSTEM: 6-round cylinder

AT THE VERY start of the 1970s, the double-action revolver was still the firearm of choice with most law enforcement agencies. But the arms manufacturer Sturm, Ruger & Co. (often just called Ruger) did not manufacture one. To correct the situation, Ruger introduced the Security Six and Speed Six revolvers. The Security Six can be shot in single-action mode or in double-action mode, which is faster but not as accurate. To achieve Ruger's goal of building a superdurable gun, the company's engineers gave heft and strength to the frame and made the gun from high-quality treated steel, designed for long life. The pistols lived up to their reputation, and most outlast other double-action revolvers by thousands of Magnum rounds. A process called "investment casting" also helped Ruger hold down production costs, so the Security Six costs less than similar revolvers. It became a standard-issue firearm for many police agencies.

Forged of blued carbon steel and the company's proprietary Terhune stainless steel, the Security Six features adjustable rear sights. The gun has a heavy trigger pull of about fourteen pounds and significant recoil. This was one of the first modern revolver designs to feature the safety-oriented transfer-bar-based lockwork and was chambered for other types of ammunition cartridges in addition to .357 Magnum, including the .38 Special, .38 S&W, and the 9x19mm Parabellum. The design emphasizes function over form.

SMITH & WESSON MODEL 317 KIT GUN .22 PISTOL
(EIGHT-ROUND REVOLVER)
COUNTRY: USA

S&W .22 MODEL 317
Country: United States
Introduced: 1998

CALIBER: .22

WEIGHT: (empty) 12.5 ounces

BARREL LENGTH: 3 inches

FIRING SYSTEM: 8-shot cylinder

THIS IS A double-action revolver with a low weight that makes it ideal for hiking, camping, and recreational shooting. Between World War I and World War II, kit bags often had a small pistol inside—hence the name kit gun. Its lightness and small size made it an ideal gun to conceal.

This pistol fires the .22 long rifle cartridge. It is equipped with an adjustable rear sight and HiViz front sight. A hollow butt helps achieve the light weight.

SIG P228 PISTOL

COUNTRY: GERMANY/SWITZERLAND

CALIBER: 9x19mm

WEIGHT: 29.1 ounces

BARREL LENGTH: 3.9 inches

FIRING SYSTEM: 13-round box magazine

THIS COMPACT, SERVICE-TYPE pistol is manufactured by SIG Sauer. For "The Shakedown" on season two, Iain Harrison chooses this and the Browning Hi-Power pistol, along with two other pieces, for a versatility competition among six final contestants. The SIG P228 is also known as the M11 in the U.S. Army and was used by the Navy SEALs and law enforcement agencies. Schweizerische Industrie Gesellschaft created the P226 version of the pistol as an entry in the XM9 Service Pistol Trials held by the U.S. Army in 1984. A modified P228 was introduced in 1993. Because of restrictions on the exporting of firearms in Switzerland, the company entered into an agreement

SIG 228 PISTOL
Country: Germany
Introduced: 1993

with J. P. Sauer & Sohn in Germany. The gun is now also produced in Exeter, New Hampshire. The primary weapon for the State Department's Bureau of Diplomatic Security and the Bureau of Alcohol, Tobacco, and Firearms, it is also chosen by FBI agents for its fabled reliability.

With a short slide and barrel, it uses a 9x19mm Parabellum with a thirteen-round magazine; magazines of fifteen or twenty rounds outfit the SIG P226. The gun operates by the locked breech, short-recoil method developed by John Browning.

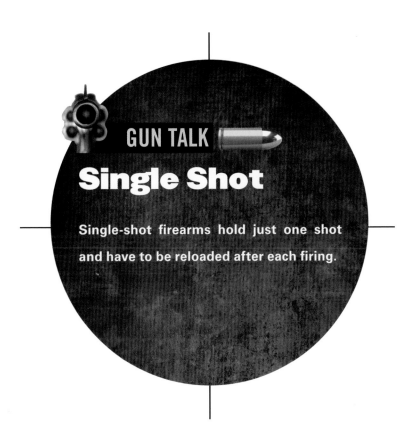

GUN TALK

Single Shot

Single-shot firearms hold just one shot and have to be reloaded after each firing.

BROWNING HI-POWER PISTOL

COUNTRY: USA

BROWNING HI-POWER PISTOL
Countries: Belgium & United States
Introduced: 1935

CALIBER: 9x19mm

WEIGHT: 2.19 pounds

BARREL LENGTH: 4.7 inches

FEED SYSTEM: 13-round 9mm cartridge or 10-round .40 S&W cartridge

ONE OF THE most widely used military pistols of all time, it was the last design that firearms inventor John Browning worked on before he died in 1926. Dieudonné Saive completed the design after his death. Browning designed the gun in response to a call from the French army for a new service pistol. It is sometimes called the HP (for Hi-Power), GP in France (for Grande Puissance, or High Yield), the P-35 (based on its introduction in 1935), or the BAP (Browning Automatic Pistol). The pistol was used by both Allied and Axis forces during World War II. Saddam Hussein carried a Hi-Power, as did Muammar Gaddafi, whose pistol was gold-plated and featured an image of his face on the grips.

A single-action 9mm semiautomatic, the gun was called Hi-Power in reference to its thirteen-round capacity, which was almost twice that of other contemporary pistols. It uses a 9x19mm Parabellum thirteen-round cartridge or a ten-round .40 S&W cartridge. The Hi-Power's trigger is not connected to the hammer. The pistol must be cocked manually before the first shot. It operates on the locked-breech, short-recoil system. The trigger pull is usually heavy. Users have complained that the external hammer has a tendency to pinch (or "bite") the web of the shooter's hand, between the thumb and forefinger, when the gun is fired.

J. J. Racaza
New Milford, New Jersey

TOP PISTOL SHOOTER J. J. Racaza was one of the shining stars on season one who made it to the final three. He is a Department of Homeland Security agent and a Double Grand Master in the USPSA/IPSC.

What have you been doing since the show ended?

Last year, 2011, was a big year for me. After *Top Shot* ended, I got back in the competition mode. The show pushed me to do a little better. And I'm more in the spotlight now that I've been on TV. So there was a little more pressure to do well. This year I placed second in the [ISSF] World Shooting Championships, and now I am ranked number two in the world.

What was your role with the Razorcat pistol, and tell me about the name?

I had some input on the design of the gun—how many holes on the compensator, for example.

I was dubbed Razor in a 2002 competition. Someone in the competition dubbed me that when I was not really known. I was kind of climbing up the ranks. I was taking out the big guys. They were trying to figure out who I was. No one knew me, so they called me "the Razor."

I never asked where it came from, but it may be because my hair looks like a razor—it's short and spiky. They say I'm very edgy when I'm shooting. Maybe I was cutting my way through to the top.

How did you get started shooting firearms?

Pistol shooting started out as just a hobby, and as a necessity for self-defense in the Philippines. Now that little hobby has catapulted me into my profession, has allowed me to meet some of the greatest people, get a dream job, meet my beautiful wife, and even "make History" on TV!

In the Philippines where I grew up, my father used to shoot in competitions, and he was always into self-defense. As soon as I was old enough and able to handle a gun, he brought me to a range and taught me the basics of firearms. I got the basic fundamentals, and he would always take me to competitions. I would start imitating him. He was always on call—he's a doctor. I was always left at the house and he would say, "You're the man of the house when I'm not here. You protect the whole house and the family." One thing led to another. He gave me a .22 single-action hot-air rifle, but that was only so I could shoot little things in the backyard and understand the concepts of gun sights, sight alignment, and trigger control. But it was all about pistols. My first competition was when I was eight years old.

Were there any surprises for you being on the show?

It's kind of funny. Coming into the show there were a couple of things that made me hesitant. Not knowing what the show was about, I thought the show might make a mockery of me and my career. I thought they might do some experimental shots that would be impossible and that it might be all luck—where it might not matter about your skill level. They had this little thing on the sign-up sheet that I'll never forget: that there were going to be mystery projectiles. I wondered what that meant, and I was always curious, but those mysterious projectiles became one of my favorites in the show. They were the bow and arrow and the throwing knives. I had zero experience with these. They didn't have anything to do with guns, shooting, lining sights whatsoever. It was just what you had and the instrument you were given.

With knife throwing, it's one of those things where you think, "This is easy. Just look at it. You just pick it up and chuck it." I think I threw about thirty-five knives at this big chunk of wood and I couldn't stick one at all. The worst part about throwing knives is you can't get frustrated; you can't get tense. Once you stick one, you can't get excited because you start affecting your muscles and all these physical things. For me, a lot of it is muscle memory. So every time I threw something at first, I was getting more tense and more frustrated. And that was one of the worst things you could do, and the expert kept telling me, "Just relax. Just take it back for a second. You're using too much muscle." And I didn't understand it until finally I stuck the first one—I just flung it there without really trying.

The only guns that looked familiar to me were the Beretta, the AR-15 or M16, and one of the revolvers—the Schofield, I think. Otherwise, every other gun that they brought out there I had never seen. The thing is, you're only given an allotted amount of time. You get the basics and then you've got to let your own skill and ability apply. As long as you get the gist of aiming and shooting it, that's all you can do. They gave you five rounds for your weapon, and you had to be ready for the next day's competition. And you're thinking, *I've never fired this gun before in my life—I don't know how the trigger feels; I don't know where it's hitting. I don't know how it's going to feel in recoil; I don't know how to load. Five rounds you're going to expect me to get this done? Wish me luck.*

You made it to the final three. Did you have any strategy?

Whatever strategy we had, no matter as a team or an individual going to each event, it was always blown out of the window. We were always going, "Okay. That didn't work. Whatever we planned yesterday doesn't matter now. Let's come up with a better strategy in the next two minutes."

My favorite was when I got to the final three and looked at all the pistols. There wasn't really a type of pistol I was familiar with. I figured the most accurate gun for me was the Schofield, and I figured, *That's the one I'm going to pick, and I'm going to put the target as far away as I can*, and I figured, *I'm going to hit it nine out of ten times.*

On a scale of one to ten, my experience with rifles was a two. I took a lot of notes on people and how they were progressing while I was on the show. It was another way to keep my sanity and prevent myself from doing something stupid. What I noticed was that the decent pistol shooters picked up the rifles a lot faster than the other way around. It seemed that there was a lot steeper learning curve for the rifle shooters compared to the pistol shooters.

To me, the rifle was the same as the pistol, with sights, alignment, and trigger control. Rifle shooters can stabilize the whole gun up to their shoulders. Shooting the pistol, it's a whole new ball game. There's not that element there to stabilize your shot. I was going to represent the pistol community.

You were asked back as an expert? How did that happen?

I think it started with them asking me, "Hey, can you come up with a couple of challenges for a pistol challenge?" And they asked if I had my own gun [the Razorcat], and they asked if I could be an expert for that. That was it.

The Razorcat is a very customized gun, designed for me and competition only.

On the other side, the whole time, the clearest, biggest memory I have is being stuck in a van blacked out, and you're being told to be quiet every five to ten seconds. That took a toll on us too. That was another part of the challenge—just keeping your sanity together.

I love to eat and I can just start grubbing. Being on the show . . . that was a joke of the producers and the camera guys, because they would try to catch me eating as much as they could, because I would try to eat about six thousand calories a day while I was out there [laughs]. I thought they were going to focus on it, because it became a huge joke as the season went along. They would keep catching me, and I would just eat. And there would be two cameras following and they would have a ball with it.

What was difficult about the show?

Everyone who came on the show had a type A personality, so they all thought they were the baddest person in the house. They each thought they were the head honcho. There were some fights here and there, but that's going to happen. You put people in a shoe box and you're going to end up head-butting with each other.

When you're in the house and you're bored and have no idea what to do, you have to put yourself into a routine, and that's what I did. I decided I was going to work out, eat, write in my notes, and take a shower—whatever I needed to do to not get bored, to not get in trouble and say something stupid to somebody else and lose focus. The most difficult thing is keeping your focus on and not being homesick.

What is your basic advice for young marksmen getting started?

Do it legally. You have to get the gun through the right channels. You can't just go in your backyard and start shooting—you have to go to some sort of range. Really start slow and maintain the basics. I compete at the highest level and I still find myself going back to the basics as much as I can. Basics are understanding sight alignment and trigger control. A lot of it is mental focus.

Shooting can get expensive—guns and bullets add up very quickly. The best is to have an unloaded weapon and do a lot of dry-firing [without ammunition]—you can do a lot; you can master sight picture, reloads, etc. And once you do that, you know what you're doing behind that firearm and then you can focus on sight alignment and trigger control.

You have to master static and dynamic shooting. Everything is moving, you're shifting your positions, and you're looking to follow up each shot with another as fast as you can. A key point is to go slow or you start to get jittery.

If you want to learn, there are plenty of local ranges around—indoor and outdoor. Any certified NRA instructor should know the basics of shooting and safety. But once you pass a certain point of basics and fundamentals you can actually practice on your own, because everyone has their own shooting style.

I've been looking more into shooting the old-school guns— the Glocks, the Smith & Wessons, the Beretta—I got exposed to the Beretta on the show. I want to compete and represent a company like that and see where that takes me. I think I can do fairly well and represent a gun company.

S & W SCHOFIELD
Country: United States
Introduced: 1875

GUN TALK

Blowback

A system of operation for self-loading firearms that obtains energy from the motion of the cartridge case as it is pushed to the rear by expanding gases created by the ignition of the propellant charge.

SMITH & WESSON .500 MAGNUM PISTOL

COUNTRY: USA

CALIBER: .50

WEIGHT: From 56 ounces to 82 ounces

BARREL LENGTH: From 4 inches to 10.5 inches

FEED SYSTEM: 5-round cylinder

INTRODUCED AT THE 2003 Shooting, Hunting, Outdoor Trade (SHOT) Show, this massive double-action, five-shot revolver was built on S&W's largest frame to fire the .500 Magnum cartridge. As might be expected, the gun has a huge recoil; its high-energy blast is capable of taking down big game. At one point the .44 Magnum that Dirty Harry used was the biggest pistol and produced a nine-hundred-foot-per-pound charge of muzzle energy from a standard load. This gun produces twenty-six hundred feet per pound with its heaviest load.

The special X-Frame was specifically designed to handle the .50-caliber cartridge. Designers had to develop a strong barrel-to-frame connection and precise cylinder alignment. The gun features a muzzle brake and recoil compensator. These are fitted to the muzzle of a firearm to reduce recoil and redirect propellant gases.

Locked Breech, Short Recoil

On firearms of this type, the slide and barrel are locked together for a few millimeters of rearward movement, after which the barrel is cammed down at the rear. By this time the bullet has left the barrel and the pressure has dropped to safe levels, whereupon the slide completes the rearward stroke, ejecting the spent cartridge. The recoil spring then propels the slide forward, stripping a round from the magazine, and in the last few millimeters of forward movement the barrel is cammed upward, locking the slide and barrel together again.

1875 REMINGTON REVOLVER

COUNTRY: USA

CALIBER: .45

WEIGHT: 2 pounds, 9 ounces

BARREL LENGTH: 7.5 inches

FEED SYSTEM: 6-round cylinder

REMINGTON ARMS DEVELOPED this single-action gun based on its popular Remington Model 1858. Also called the Improved Army or Frontier Army revolver, the gun competed with the Colt Single-Action Army line. Because Colt had already secured contracts with the U.S. Army, Remington had to search for sales elsewhere. Frank James used one throughout his life as an outlaw. The form features a fluted cylinder, walnut grip panels, and a blued or nickel-plated finish with a case-hardened hammer and loading gate, and a lanyard ring. Manufactured with three different chamberings for .44, .44-40, and .45 caliber.

SMITH & WESSON 686 REVOLVER

COUNTRY: USA

CALIBER: .357

WEIGHT: 2 pounds, 12 ounces

BARREL LENGTH: 2.5 inches, 3 inches, 4 inches, and 6 inches

FEED SYSTEM: 6- or 7-round cylinder

IN SEASON THREE, episode seven, the S&W 686 was the gun of choice for a couple of trick shots. The remaining competitors blasted at three beer bottles from thirty feet holding the double-action S&W 686 upside down and pulling the trigger with their pinkie. They also had to shoot water jugs with this revolver while blindfolded. There have been many models of the 686. These guns are built on S&W's durable Large Frame (or L-Frame). The guns are developed to withstand heavy use and are popular among law enforcement personnel and hunters.

This is a six- or seven-shot revolver chambered for the .357 Magnum. In 1988, the Classic Hunter, with its six-inch barrel, was introduced. In 1989, the Black Stainless (with four- and six-inch barrels) came out in a limited run of five thousand. Other versions include the National Security Special, with its shorter three- and four-inch barrels; the Target Champion, with its adjustable trigger stop; and the Power Port, with a ported six-inch barrel. (Ported barrels have holes in them, reducing muzzle jump and recoil, allowing for faster shots, and keeping the barrel on target. On the negative side, ported barrels can potentially blind the shooter at night and possibly spray ammo debris, and gases from the port can leave powder residue on the front sights, making it difficult to clean.)

TOP SHOT CHALLENGE CLOSE-UP

"Down the Tubes" Challenge:
SEASON ONE

THE SETUP: The team challenge is designed to test both the speed and accuracy of the competitors' marksmanship with a pistol. Seven tubes of decreasing diameter are placed on the range, starting at four inches and going all the way down to an inch and a half. The smallest target is like hitting a quarter. The distance is twenty-five feet. Each team has to rank its members by skill and assign them a tube. Starting with the largest tube, the first team member shoots once to get a bullet through the tube, shattering a Plexiglas cover on the end. If the player misses one shot, he or she has to step back behind the line and let the rest of the team go before trying again. Whichever team successfully fires through all seven tubes in the fastest time wins the challenge, safe from elimination.

The losing team from the last challenge gets to eliminate a player from the winning team. The decreasing tube size makes accuracy more and more difficult.

THE OUTCOME: The Blue Team wins this challenge, although they feel handicapped by James Sinclair, who is an experienced rifle shooter but has very little experience with handguns. During practice, James has a difficult time hitting the targets. The Red Team is confident going in, as they have several members with pistol experience. During the competition, however, three of the Red Team shooters, who were expected to perform well, miss several times. Bill Carns and Brad Engmann each take two shots to hit the target, and Frank Campana takes three shots. Every competitor on the Blue Team hits the target on the first shot except for James, who takes two shots. The Blue Team wins with a time of two minutes, seven seconds. The Red Team's time is two minutes, thirty-four seconds.

THE ELIMINATION: The Red Team's members select Frank and Brad. Frank has missed the most shots, and some teammates are frustrated with Brad. Although Brad is known for his marksmanship with small firearms, he has not performed, and he is annoying other teammates with his constant explaining of why he was underperforming.

ELIMINATION CHALLENGE: Competitors have to hit targets while descending down a zip line. Whoever hits the most targets wins. Frank, who felt uncomfortable shooting a Beretta, loses the challenge.

WALTHER P38 PISTOL

COUNTRY: GERMANY

CALIBER: 9x19mm Parabellum

WEIGHT: 1 pound, 12 ounces

BARREL LENGTH: 4.9 inches

FEED SYSTEM: 8-round detachable single-stack magazine

MIKE HUGHES AND Gary Quesenberry compete with this iconic German World War II pistol in an elimination toward the end of season three. Shooting from thirty-five feet, the marksmen fire at separate sets of thirty-six targets holding up eight planks in a vertical frame. They work from the bottom up, with thirty rounds preloaded in their magazines.

Carl Walther GmbH Sportwaffen, or Walther, a German arms manufacturer for more than a hundred years, created the P38, the first double-action pistol made in 9mm. The P38 was first produced under Nazi rule starting in 1939, and became the main service pistol for Hitler's forces in World War II. Walther received many patents for the unique features: the breech block, extractor, firing pin, loaded-chamber indicator, and the breech-locking system.

This 9mm pistol features short recoil, detachable magazines, a double-action trigger, and a loaded chamber indicator. The Walther P38 has a five-inch barrel with a front blade post and rear notch sights. P38s from WWII were manufactured of steel, but after the war they were constructed of aluminum alloy to reduce weight. One unique feature of note: Walther P38 has right-side ejection and spits out spent cases over the shooter's left shoulder.

Center fire versus Rimfire

These are terms for ammunition cartridges. In a center-fire cartridge, a primer is located in the center of the cartridge case head, while in a rimfire, the primer is a separate replaceable component. Pulling the trigger releases a hammer, which strikes the percussion cap and ignites the explosive primer.

Kelly Bachand

Age: 22
Home: Kent, Washington
Season One Contestant

BACHAND IS A college student earning a degree in electrical engineering from the University of Washington. He started shooting when he got a Red Ryder BB gun for his fifth Christmas. He began shooting in long-range rifle competitions four years ago. He made the Under 21 U.S. National Rifle Team in 2006, and by 2007, he won the gold for the team. In 2009, winning gold as an individual, he became the youngest person and first American to win the Canadian Open Target Rifle Championship.

What did you enjoy most about being on the show?

I really enjoyed the sniper rifle challenge that I got to do in the first episode. It was an elimination challenge, and it was the only time in the whole show where I got to use updated equipment—a Remington 700. We weren't using a World War II replica or stuff that's been sitting on a shelf somewhere, and it wasn't a $50 Mosin-Nagant. The Mosin-Nagant is the crappiest rifle that exists, in my opinion. The best thing to do with it is bury it in the ground and leave it there. I bought one for $50 once and I couldn't hit a two-foot target at fifty yards. I had never shot a sniper rifle before. I thought, *This is cool. I ought to buy one.*

I was up against Mike Seeklander. That competition was in my favor. I smiled when I saw it. If you watch the episode closely . . . I had fun with it in the practice. I shot a smiley face at the target, because I didn't need all the bullets to practice. In the elimination, they gave me a rifle with a bipod and a scope, and the targets were huge and really close. I was thinking honestly that I could probably do this left-handed.

I also enjoyed using the Beretta Xtrema 12-gauge. That was really cool. That shotgun had no recoil. If you use an ordinary shotgun, you can get a big bruise on your arm [if you don't hold it correctly]. That was not the case with this one at all. It was awesome. I don't know how much they cost, but I really want one.

What were some of the most difficult challenges?

The poker wheel challenge was awful. Even though I won, I didn't win by hits. I had the most misses in that challenge, but Andre made an enormous error by shooting the wrong cards completely. I felt bittersweet about that. I felt like, *Wow, I'm still here, but I really don't deserve it.*

The Kentucky long rifle was also an awful challenge. In practice, we only got three shots, and three bullets is not a whole lot. The rifle has got a weird trigger. You shoot it, and a half second later it goes off. It's got a flintlock, so there's an explosion in your face. It's really different from other rifles.

What did you enjoy about being with the other competitors?

I became good friends with many of them. I went to J. J. Racaza's wedding after the show. I felt really close to Tara. We'd be up really, really late in the house when there's nothing to do, and we'd run into each other in the kitchen. I've visited Chris Cerino and met his family. Peter Palma is awesome. I've seen him a couple times since. He's hilarious. I've seen Caleb Giddings; he's moved up to the Pacific Northwest. And I've enjoyed hanging out with Iain Harrison, who lives in Oregon.

I even patched things up somewhat with Bill Carns. Bill was pretty upset with me. I had a kind of foot-in-mouth experience with him [making a joke about his ex-wife]. It was twisted out of proportion. He was pretty immature about it. As he was leaving the show, though, I slipped him a note, again apologizing. They didn't show that on the show. They didn't even show me shaking his hand. But he did shake my hand. When I got home from the show a couple weeks later, I had a long e-mail apology from him. He said, "Hey, I'm so sorry." It seemed quite genuine. So I went on his radio show, and we had fun.

How did you grow or change from being on the show?

You can't have a life experience like that and not have it change you slightly. I was really trying to be modest on the show [and learning to do that]. Modesty was something I had to work on. I wasn't always that way. In 2005 and 2006, I made it onto a state rifle-shooting team. I won the Washington state championship two years in a row, and I thought I was the coolest thing in the world. But I [verbally] blasted some of my teammates. I threw them under the bus. I was really arrogant and narcissistic. I got kicked off the team for it. Ever since then, I've felt like, Wow, I was a total jerk. I was unable to win without pissing people off. I was unable to lose without pissing people off. So one of the things I tried to showcase on the show, and off the show, was that I am a very humble, approachable guy. I think there's a lot to be said for that.

What is your advice for amateur marksmen?

Always have a willingness to learn and an access to knowledge. I think to be the best in the world you also need natural talent. Some of the best advice I can give is, Never be done learning. I never think I'm done learning. And I'm never so arrogant or proud to not take someone's advice and at least try it. If you can always just assume there's a little more to learn, then you're always in a place where you can better yourself. But the minute you say you're as good as you can get, you've peaked and plateaued; you're not going to get any better. Keep an open mind, keep your ego in check, and surround yourself with skilled people who you can learn from. That's a great tool.

The great thing about shooting sports, especially for young shooters, is that there is a big community among the older shooters who want to pass down the sport. They really have an attitude of, "We have to keep the sport alive. We have to teach the younger generation how to shoot." Because of that, a younger shooter who is enthusiastic and actually tries and listens and applies things that he's taught will be handed things—[lessons, weapons, etc.]—that's just how the community is. I've been the recipient of that.

What are your plans for the future?

I will finish my college degree in June. I have an internship with an aerospace company. Hopefully I'll start working for them or another company. I plan to get engaged soon after, and then get married. I'll be shooting until I can't see anymore, and after that I'll have to start using scopes. I'll absolutely keep competing. I went to Australia this past year for three weeks for the world championship of long-range rifle shooting, but since then I've been working sixty to seventy hours a week. I've been working my way through school, working anywhere from one to three part-time jobs. As soon as I have some time, I want to go snowboarding. I've never done that. Shooting-wise, I really want to get into some three-gun competitions—it's rifle, pistol, shotgun. You run around and shoot targets really fast. In fact, I bought all the guns to do it. I've got essentially everything I need to do it, but I need to find the time to do it.

BERETTA XTREMA2
Country: Italy
Introduced: 2004

SVI INFINITY SIGHT TRACKER .40 PISTOL
COUNTRY: USA

CALIBER: .40
WEIGHT: 2.25 pounds
BARREL LENGTH: 5 inches

IN A *TOP Shot* speed challenge, competitors in season three use this race gun custom-made by Strayer-Voigt Inc. Each marksman fires at targets that randomly appear behind twelve four-inch holes in an eight-foot-diameter board wheel at thirty-five feet. Shooters also use it in the season three finale in the Call Your Shot competition.

Strayer-Voigt is most famous for its hybrid series of pistols that are marketed under the brand name Infinity Firearms. In 1994, Sandy Strayer and Michael Voigt, a professional shooter and gunsmith, respectively, formed Strayer-Voigt to produce modular-frame 1911s. The lower grip and trigger guard are made of a fiber-reinforced plastic and form a separate component from the metal upper portion of the frame. They are made in a variety of calibers, including .38 Super, 9x23mm Winchester, .40 S&W, .45 ACP, 10mm auto, and .357 SIG. The pistols generally hold about twice as many rounds of ammunition per magazine as traditional 1911s. They are one of the more expensive pistols on the market, costing $4,000 and up, but are distinguished by their accuracy.

H&K SP89 PISTOL

COUNTRY: GERMANY

CALIBER: 9x19mm Parabellum

WEIGHT: 4.4 pounds empty

BARREL LENGTH: 4.5 inches

FEED SYSTEM: 15- or 30-round magazine

ON THE THIRD season, the final five marksmen were strapped to a carnival-style contraption and shot the powerful and compact SP89 pistol at targets on a wheel, while moving through the air upside down and being spun in a loop thirty-three feet in the air. Heckler & Koch manufactures the gun, which is a civilian semiautomatic version of an MP5K, the shortened pistol version of the MP5 submachine gun. After developing a successful line of automatic rifles, H&K made a family of small arms. The SP89s were imported to the United States between 1989 and 1993, but President Bill Clinton halted importation by executive order in 1993.

The H&K SP89 is a large-frame pistol with high accuracy. It is suited for target shooting and small-game hunting. For low recoil the pistol uses a delayed-roller, locked-bolt system common to many H&K firearms. The SP89 comes with an optional laser sight.

STEYR SPP (SPECIAL PURPOSE PISTOL)

COUNTRY: AUSTRIA

WEIGHT: 3.1 pounds fully loaded with 15-round magazine

BARREL LENGTH: 12⅗ inches overall length

FEED SYSTEM: 15- or 30-round magazine

IN A SEASON-THREE elimination challenge, Mike Hughes and Alex Charvat blasted the SPP as they were propelled backward down a zip line at twenty miles per hour, fifteen feet off the ground. Produced by Steyr Mannlicher, the semiautomatic Steyr SPP is the civilian version of the Steyr TMP (Tactical Machine Pistol), and it was designed as a close-range weapon with minimum recoil.

Engineered from state-of-the-art molded synthetic material called DCEF 1313, the firearm features a lower section housing moving components (trigger and safety mechanism) and an upper section with the bolt and barrel subassemblies. The SPP employs a delayed blowback and short-recoil operation, featuring a rotating barrel, designed to increase accuracy in rapid fire compared to simple blowback pistols. The bolt action causes some muzzle flip. It has a heavy trigger pull of ten or twelve pounds. Sights are molded into the top and are not adjustable.

The Kentucky Long Rifle and Kentucky Flintlock Pistol

From the American Revolution to the War of 1812, the flint-lock-fired Kentucky long rifles and pistols played a key role in America's fight to gain and keep its independence. At the start of the American Revolution, the Continental Congress formed the Continental Army to coordinate the efforts of the thirteen colonies. With George Washington as its commander in chief, the army enlisted riflemen (many who were tradesmen and farmers) from Pennsylvania, Delaware, Maryland, and Virginia— often armed with their own Kentucky long rifles and pistols. The Continental Congress in 1775 passed a resolution calling for six companies of expert riflemen. Most came armed with firearms that were civilian-made, handcrafted by individual gunsmiths.

Similar to an early *Top Shot* competition, these companies of riflemen occasionally put on exhibitions of marksmanship for the townspeople. A spectator at one such demonstration in the 1700s described it: "[T]wo brothers in the company took a piece of board, five inches broad and seven inches long, with a bit of white paper about the size of a dollar nailed in the center, and while one of them supported this board perpendicularly be-tween his knees, the other at a distance of upwards of sixty yards and without any kind of a rest, shot eight bullets succes-sively through the board, and spared his brother's thighs."

The long rifle exhibited amazing accuracy over the musket. In 1777, sharpshooter Tim Murphy shot and killed British officers Sir Francis Clerke and General Simon Fraser at three hundred yards. In 1778 at the Battle of Boonesborough, Kentucky, Daniel Boone killed a British officer at around 250 yards. There was a trade-off: the long rifles took much longer to load. It took a full minute to load compared to the musket's twenty seconds.

The weapons weren't called "Kentucky" at first, but they gained that name over time as marksmen from Kentucky built a reputation for winning battles with these guns. Perhaps the most famous battle win attributed to the Kentucky long rifle was during the War of 1812. In 1815, General Andrew Jackson gathered together an army of Kentuckians armed with the rifles and stopped the British at the Battle of New Orleans. (Though the war was officially over, speculation ran that had the British secured a route, it might have started up again. . . .)

As our country pushed westward, frontiersmen depended on the long rifle for survival, mostly for hunting big game, such as elk, buffalo, mule deer, and grizzly bears.

KENTUCKY FLINTLOCK PISTOL

COUNTRY: USA

CALIBER: .50

WEIGHT: 1 pound, 7 ounces

BARREL LENGTH: 10 inches

FEED SYSTEM: Manually place each ball

MADE BY THE same gunsmiths who made the Kentucky flintlock rifles, this pistol was popular in the late eighteenth and early nineteenth centuries. The name "Kentucky" comes from there being two thousand riflemen from Kentucky who were responsible for winning the Battle of New Orleans (which was fought after the signing of the treaty that officially ended the War of 1812 between the young Republic and England).

Loading the flintlock pistol requires measuring a specific amount of gunpowder (about twenty-five grains) to fire a .50-caliber lead ball. The ball has to be rammed down the barrel to sit firmly against the powder charge. The shooter also has to put in primer powder. There is a delay in firing the pistol (which caused Kelly Bachand some consternation) created by the primer powder igniting and then igniting the main powder charge.

HK MARK 23

COUNTRY: GERMANY

HECKLER & KOCH USP TACTICAL .45
COUNTRY: GERMANY
INTRODUCED: 1993

CALIBER: .45 ACP (automatic Colt pistol)

WEIGHT: 2.7 pounds empty, 3.2 pounds loaded

BARREL LENGTH: 5.9 inches

FEED SYSTEM: 12-round magazine

USED AS AN offensive handgun for the United States Special Operations Command (USSOCOM) in the 1990s, this match-grade semiautomatic pistol provides a laser aiming module (LAM) and a suppressor (or silencer). Known for its remarkable stopping power and exceptional durability in harsh environments, it is also relatively big and heavy.

The gun features a polygonal barrel design, ambidextrous safety, and magazine releases, and the ability to shoot high-pressure match cartridges. The firearm was tested and found to be capable of firing tens of thousands of rounds without a barrel change.

WEBLEY MARK VI

COUNTRY: GREAT BRITAIN

CALIBER: .445 Webley

WEIGHT: 2.4 pounds unloaded

BARREL LENGTH: 6-inch barrel

FEED SYSTEM: 6-round cylinder

THE BRITISH ARMED forces issued this as its service pistol from 1887 to 1963. The Mark VI is perhaps the most famous, introduced in 1915 during World War I. The Mark VI became known as the Boer War model because of its extensive use by officers during that conflict. A bayonet was developed for the pistol as well as speed-loader devices (the Prideaux Device and the Watson design). The Hong Kong, Singapore, and London police forces all depended on Webley revolvers.

The piece is a top-break, double-action revolver with a fixed front blade and rear notch, and automatic extraction. When the shooter opens this pistol to reload, the automatic extractor removes the brass casing of fired ammunition after the ammunition has been fired. Shooting at .445 made this one of the largest, most-powerful revolvers ever produced.

FN FIVE-SEVEN
(5.7MM)
COUNTRY: BELGIUM

CALIBER: FN 5.7x28mm

WEIGHT: 1.3 pounds empty, 1.6 pounds loaded

BARREL LENGTH: 8.2 inches

FEED SYSTEM: 20-round magazine standard

DESIGNED AND MANUFACTURED by FN Herstal in Belgium, this gun is named after the 5.7mm bullet it fires. The semiautomatic is used by military and law enforcement in more than forty countries. Civilians purchase them for self-defense and target shooting. The gun saw action in the Afghanistan war and the Libyan revolution. The weapon was developed in response to a request from NATO to develop personal defense weapons (PDWs) that were to be used for personal protection in last-resort situations when endangered by an enemy.

This semiautomatic features a hidden hammer and delayed blow-back. It is chambered for FN's 5.7×28mm ammunition. It is constructed largely of polymer, but trigger, spring, barrel, and other parts are all made of steel. With a very light weight of just over a pound, the firearm uses a bullet that can penetrate certain types of body armor, including Kevlar protective vests.

Maggie Reese
Chino, California
Occupation: Professional Shooter
Season Two Competitor—Eliminated: Week Four

"I **LOVE SHOOTING** against bigger, stronger, tougher men." Don't be fooled by her stunning looks—Maggie Reese is a professional multigun champion with numerous national titles under her belt. With thirteen years of experience in the shooting sports, Maggie has made herself a name in the gun community at home and abroad (in international competitions). And when it comes to *Top Shot*, she's not afraid of the competition. "I love it when they underestimate me, and I love when I have an opportunity to prove myself."

What are you currently up to?

I'm a full-time competition shooter. I did that before the series and I continue to do that now. I work with different companies within the firearms industry doing R & D, and product development and testing—primarily through my competition but also through instruction. I always wanted to figure out how to travel and see the world. But I love shooting and it's taken me all over and given me so many experiences. That's how I got on *Top Shot*. I'm steamrolling ahead, and great things just keep coming.

How did you get involved with shooting?

I started when I was eighteen. There were guns in the household. It wasn't something that I was interested in. It was at about age eighteen that my dad took me out. I didn't see myself as an athletic person or a competitive or outdoors person. Nothing appealed to me about guns at first. But from the moment my dad took me out and pushed me and said, "Let's just do this and see if you like it," I found I really enjoyed it. It was something I could do with my dad on the weekends in the summer and spend time outdoors and have fun and meet other people. It grew from there. I did it just as a hobby up until about four years ago, and then something clicked and I said, "You know what? I don't want to do this just as a hobby. I want to compete and do more." It pushed me to something new.

What did you enjoy most about *Top Shot*?

Being on the show is a totally different level. It's the first time I truly relied on myself, because I didn't have my usual support system. I enjoyed the challenge of being thrown into a situation and not knowing what to expect and not having my usual people to rely on. It was just myself. Somebody hands you something that you're not familiar with, and in the moment, in the panic, with all the adrenaline, you've got to rely on instinct.

I really loved being on the show. All of us who were on the show were experience junkies—we just want to look for the next new thing and just get out of our comfort zone and try something that not everybody has the opportunity to do.

The paintball competition was fun. That was a curveball. We didn't see that in the first season.

We had a challenge where we had to run up a hill and blow up an ammo dump. That was a fairly steep hill. I'm not a runner by nature. I'm not a strong person. My partner on that was Chris Tilley, and he took off and said, "Okay, we're just going to have a nice easy pace and get to our positions so we can make a good shot." He took off at what I guess he thought was a nice easy pace, and I was way far back. I remember him looking back at me and saying, "C'mon, C'mon." I got more feedback about that episode than any other from complete strangers teasing me, saying, "Wow, you are not a runner."

What was it like being one of the few women on the show?

That part didn't concern me. Shooting in the sports industry—it's so male-dominated to begin with, and I'm so used to being on the range, and going to competitions and . . . I'm used to people coming up to me and saying, "Are you lost?" "No, I'm here. I'm a competitor; I'm going to do this." I'm used to this environment. So being one of two women didn't bother me. And people are usually very welcoming. They love to see women out there, because there are so few of us. They're really encouraging and welcoming, and that's the way it was on the show.

Do you get recognized?

Surprisingly, I never get recognized. I've talked to other contestants and they get recognized in public all the time. I never do. I've gotten a lot of positive feedback on Facebook and a lot of e-mails internationally. People saying, "Wow, my wife, my daughter, my girlfriend saw you on TV and they just got so inspired about shooting because of what they saw another woman do." And that's really been the fun part of it for me. Every couple of months the show seems to premiere in different countries, and then I get a whole new resurgence of e-mails. Women ask, "How can I shoot; where can I go?" I'm excited that they find a new sport that they're really passionate about.

What was the hardest part of being on the show?

I think the hardest part was not being able to call home to family at the end of the day and say, "Look what I did," and, "This is what we're going to do tomorrow." The hardest part is being cut off from the rest of the world—no TV, no telephone, no Internet, and no newspaper, and no family. That's really hard.

Elimination is hard to go through. You so badly want to be there. We had all been through so much, going through the whole casting process and the challenges you have. Taking time off of work and families—you don't want to leave before the party's over.

There are different reasons why you vote. People sometimes say, "Just make the vote performance-based," but do you do performance-based on one challenge, or do you look at multiple challenges? Do you give someone a bye because they just had a bad day or do you say, "No, it doesn't matter that you did good yesterday; all that matters is today." How do you figure out how to make it superfair? There is no way.

There was one really hard moment where I had to be the deciding factor—a tiebreaker. And I ended up picking Jay. There's so many things that you bring into it.

My elimination challenge was in archery. I was unfamiliar with it, and it took a lot of upper-body strength and technique and muscles that I wasn't used to using. It was a challenge mentally, because I wasn't familiar with the equipment, but it was a challenge physically as well.

You're always thinking that you're on TV, and you're thinking, Just don't let me be a jackass right now.

What did you do with your downtime?

We had a fun group of people. We made our own activities. We had a fly problem in the house from the food and the trash and the doors being left open. So for a while we went on a fly-killing spree, and we tried to see who could collect the most bodies. You had to have a confirmed kill. You can see that competitive nature just carries on into everything.

What are your favorite guns to use?

I shoot a lot of different divisions, and each division has a lot of different rules about the guns you can use. I really like an unlimited or open division, which allows you to make any modification you'd like to make to a pistol, rifle, or shotgun. I like to push the technology or the envelope and make things better and faster and stronger and more powerful. An example of that would be what you saw later on in season two. You saw the Razorcat. That's called an "open handgun," and I shoot a gun that's similar to that. I like to shoot something like that, that's tricked out. Every bell and whistle that you can have—that's what I want on my gun.

What advice can you give to young marksmen?

Just go out there, and every opportunity you have to try something new, take it. If you can, go to a gun range or a gun club. If you can put yourself in a position to meet new people and try out different weapons, that's the best thing to do—to always push the envelope and get your hands on things that are unfamiliar to you. It will help you in your personal shooting, and definitely help you if you find yourself in a situation like being on *Top Shot*.

GUN TALK

Bore

The inside of a gun's barrel through which ammunition travels.

RIFLES

ALMOST EVERY CONTESTANT who has appeared has had some experience with a rifle, firing it either for target practice, hunting, or military training. In season two, every marksman had a .22 rifle at home and was comfortable picking off targets with the Ruger 10/22 semiautomatic in a shooting gallery competition. "The .22 rifle is the first gun many young marksmen learn to shoot," says Colby Donaldson. "It's accurate, has virtually no recoil—and the ammo? Dirt cheap. This weapon levels the playing field and gets back to basics."

Traditional rifles are made of the stock (the part of the gun to which the barrel and firing mechanism are attached), the barrel, the trigger and hammer assembly, the bolt assembly that contains the firing pin, and a magazine tube for the ammunition. Most semiautomatic rifles also have a buffer assembly made of a rod and spring, designed to reduce recoil.

Compared to handguns, rifles are long guns (the Ruger 10/22 measures thirty-seven inches in length, compared to a 1911 Colt handgun at 8.25 inches), and rifles take two hands to fire. As a shooter, you prop the butt of a rifle on your chest at the shoulder. With the dominant eye, you must align the front and rear sights perfectly. There are four common shooting positions for the rifle (as well as a shotgun and handgun): standing, kneeling, sitting, and prone. In the episode nine elimination challenge on season two of *Top Shot*, Jay Lim and Jamie Franks have to fire the M1 Garand rifle from both kneeling and prone positions. As with all firearms, trigger squeeze, body position, and breathing are essential.

Rifles are used for firing longer distances than handguns, so marksmen have to pay more attention to the effects of wind and consider how the lead will drop as it hurtles over a long distance. This was certainly a factor as season one competitors were trying to hit a 125-yard target with an old Kentucky long rifle.

The word *rifle* refers to the rifling, or grooving, cut into the barrel walls. The grooving imparts a spin to the bullet that gives it aerodynamics in the same way that a properly thrown football flies through the air. Rifling dates back to the fifteenth century. In the eighteenth century, the English mathematician Benjamin Robins realized that an elongated bullet would travel more easily through the air than a musket ball.

Top Shot competitors have experienced a range of rifles from throughout history. In season one, shooters were firing the Kentucky long rifle, loaded through the muzzle with gunpowder and ball. Muzzle-loading rifles were the weapon of sharpshooters in the American Revolution. In the 1860s, the loading technique improved with the introduction of breech-loading rifles with bolt-action mechanisms. Season two of *Top Shot* kicked off with a competition designed to emulate sharpshooters during the Civil War. Using the Sharps rifle, contestants fired at a target two hundred yards downrange. The innovation of magazine feeding sped the loading process with rifles. The Spencer repeating rifle was the first magazine-fed firearm to achieve widespread success in the American Civil War. Contestants have all enjoyed using the latest high-tech, high-powered rifles as well. In season three, shooters competed with the ultramodern, lightweight LaRue Tactical OBR (Optimized Battle Rifle). "This is essentially a battle rifle that has been optimized to make it into an accurate sniper rifle," says Colby Donaldson. "It's popular with special ops." Sharpshooters agree that precision firing of any rifle—from any era—still comes back to the fundamentals of aim, stance, trigger pull, and breathing, and only mastering these basics will lead a competitor to becoming a Top Shot.

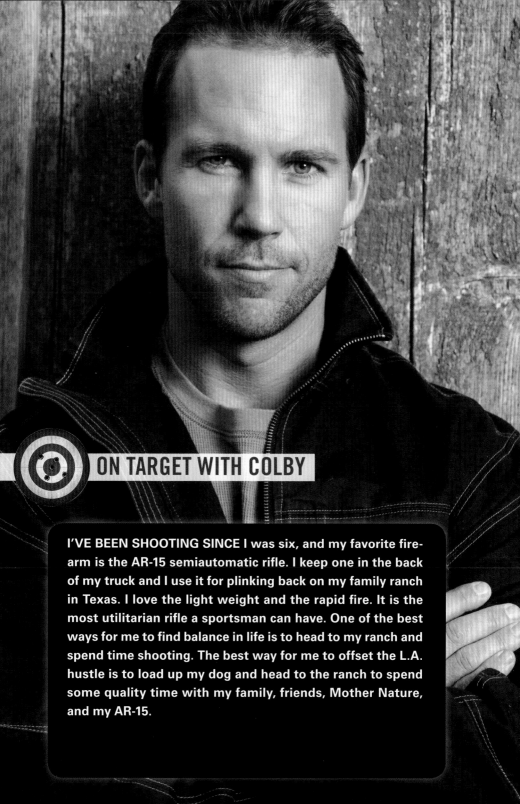

ON TARGET WITH COLBY

I'VE BEEN SHOOTING SINCE I was six, and my favorite fire-arm is the AR-15 semiautomatic rifle. I keep one in the back of my truck and I use it for plinking back on my family ranch in Texas. I love the light weight and the rapid fire. It is the most utilitarian rifle a sportsman can have. One of the best ways for me to find balance in life is to head to my ranch and spend time shooting. The best way for me to offset the L.A. hustle is to load up my dog and head to the ranch to spend some quality time with my family, friends, Mother Nature, and my AR-15.

SPRINGFIELD 1903

COUNTRY: USA

M1903 SPRINGFIELD
Country: United States
Introduced: 1903

CALIBER: .30-03 and .30-06

WEIGHT: 8.67 pounds

BARREL LENGTH: 24 inches

FEEDING SYSTEM: 5-round standard or a variant 25-round stripper clip. Internal box magazine

SEASON ONE CONTESTANTS kick off the *Top Shot* series with a rifle relay using rifles from different eras, including the Springfield. Mike Seeklander, an ex-Marine and a senior instructor at the United States Shooting Academy, struggles with the weapon, missing his hundred-yard target a large number of times. His performance sends him to elimination. Adopted as a U.S. military bolt-action rifle in 1903, the Springfield was heavily used in World War I and into World War II. Soldiers used it as a sniper rifle through the Korean War and into the Vietnam War. The U.S. War Department developed the rifle, which combined features of three other rifles—the Spanish Mauser 93, the Krag, and the German Mauser 98. The United States started to produce it at the federally owned Springfield Armory. Over time, the guns were produced by several manufacturers, including by the Smith Corona typewriter company, which helped meet demand in World War II. The gun appears in "The Short Happy Life of Francis Macomber," by Ernest Hemingway; *From Here to Eternity*, by James Jones; and in the film *Saving Private Ryan*.

This bolt-action, five-shot, magazine-fed rifle has a maximum range for a ball cartridge of 2.77 miles, but the rifle is sighted for twenty-five hundred yards. It can shoot about twenty shots per minute.

SVT-40
(RUSSIAN SEMIAUTOMATIC RIFLE)
COUNTRY: RUSSIA

CALIBER: 7.62 mm

WEIGHT: 8.5 pounds

BARREL LENGTH: 24.6 inches

FEEDING SYSTEM: 10-round detachable magazine

THE FULL NAME is a mouthful: Samozaryadnaya Vintovka Tokareva, Obrazets 1940 goda. The gun appeared on the first episode of season one in the four-gun challenge. In 1935, Stalin held a design competition to build a semiautomatic infantry rifle, and ultimately Fedor Tokarev's design was chosen. An improved follow-up design to the SVT-38, the SVT-40 was a predominant weapon on the Eastern Front during World War II. It continued to be a key weapon on the battlefields in the Korean War, Vietnam War, and Cuban Revolution. This short-stroke, gas-operated weapon has a spring-loaded piston above the barrel and a tilting bolt.

GUN TALK

Carbine

A lightweight rifle with a short barrel. Carbine comes from the Old French word *carabine*, referring to the unique firearm used by the *carabin*, or the mounted musketeers of the 1600s.

MOSIN-NAGANT
(RUSSIAN MILITARY RIFLE)
COUNTRY: RUSSIA

CALIBER: 7.62x54mmR (rimfire)

WEIGHT: 8.8 pounds

BARREL LENGTH: 28.7 inches

FEEDING SYSTEM: 5-round, nondetachable magazine

ANOTHER OF THE four rifles used on the first episode of *Top Shot*, season one, the Mosin-Nagant was a Russian military rifle developed as a result of Russia's efforts to modernize its Imperial Army in the 1880s. Part of the plan included equipping soldiers with magazine-fed multiround weapons. A special military commission came to a split decision over two designs—one submitted by Sergei Ivanovich Mosin, an Imperial Army captain, and one submitted by Leon Nagant, a Belgian. The Mosin-Nagant combines elements of both weapons. Imperial Army infantrymen relied on Mosin-Nagants in World War I. The weapon was heavily used during the Russian Revolution, and Finland (which was a grand duchy in the Russian Empire until 1917) employed the rifle in its military. The Mosin-Nagant continued to be the standard-issue weapon for Soviet troops in World War II. Fighters in Poland, Czechoslovakia, China, Syria, Iraq, Afghanistan, Palestine, and Syria have all used Mosin-Nagants.

This bolt-action, internal-magazine-fed military rifle fires 7.62mm ammunition fed from an integral single-stack magazine. The rifle has a maximum range of around three kilometers, but was capable of effective, aimed fire out to ranges of only four to five hundred meters. The weapon is striker-fired, and the striker was cocked on the bolt-open action.

M14
(AMERICAN AUTOMATIC RIFLE)
COUNTRY: USA

CALIBER: 7.62x51mm NATO and .308 Winchester

WEIGHT: 9.8 pounds empty

BARREL LENGTH: 22 inches

FEEDING SYSTEM: 20-round detachable magazine box, or 50-round coil magazine

THE FOURTH WEAPON used in the first challenge of season one of *Top Shot*. Designed in 1954, the rifle was intended to take the place of four separate weapons systems in the U.S. military—the M1 rifle, the M1 carbine, the M3 "Grease Gun," and the M19 Browning Automatic Rifle, but the cartridge was too powerful for the submachine gun role and too heavy to replace a light machine gun like the Browning. The rifle was relied on by infantrymen in the Vietnam War, but it was criticized for being too long and heavy for maneuvering through the thick brush of Vietnam. Production ended in 1964.

The American selective automatic rifle fires 7.62x51mm NATO and the commercial .308 Winchester rounds. The 7.62 rifle cartridge was developed as standard for small arms among NATO countries in the 1950s. The weapon can shoot 700–750 rounds per minute. The effective range is five hundred yards, or eight hundred yards when fitted with a scope.

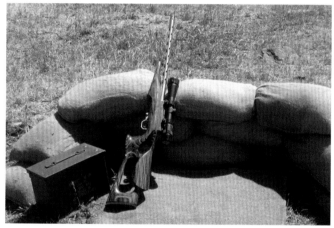

Iain Harrison
Age: 42
Sherwood, Oregon
Season One Winner

HARRISON IS A British-born construction manager who served as a recon platoon commander in the British army. He placed second in the USPSA 2009 MGM Ironman, and has shot everything from small service arms to 120mm antitank missiles and 30mm cannons. He placed second in trooper class at last year's Ironman, using firearms he made himself. He currently works as the media relations manager for Crimson Trace, an industry leader in laser sighting products for handguns and rail-equipped long guns.

What was the best part of being on *Top Shot*?

The opportunity was good for me and got me a whole new career. I was in construction as a construction manager before, and now I'm the media relations manager for Crimson Trace, based in Wilsonville, just south of Portland.

The show opened doors for me. I'm shooting a lot more now. I have some great sponsors who make sure I go to the matches and shoot competitively.

I get recognized all the time. I was recognized by some dude in Starbucks this morning when I was getting coffee.

I think the show addresses an untapped market. It's been very popular. It's good to see that History has the courage to put on a shooting show. It was completely untried before this, and they're reaping the rewards in terms of ratings.

What were your favorite parts of the show?

The most enjoyable part of the show was making a whole bunch of new friends. You make friends from all seasons.

My favorite weapon was the SVT-40, a Russian semiautomatic rifle used widely in World War II. It was new to me. It was interesting to see how far advanced the Russians were in their small-arms design compared to everybody else. I guess they didn't have the industrial capacity to put them into wider production.

If you went to elimination, you had more exposure to weapons. You knew that many of those weapons in elimination challenges would come around in the finale, if you made it that far. If you went to elimination and made it through it could be an advantage, because you already had one or two training sessions on those guns.

I went to one elimination with James Sinclair shooting at moving friend-or-foe targets with a TZ 99 and won. I had a lot of downtime at that point. I was getting a little bored, so I thought I might as well go. If I went and came back, it justified my position. If one of our really good shooters went up and got eliminated, then we would have been in a weaker position as a team. I wouldn't want someone like J.J. to go up against James, and then if he got eliminated we would have been a much weaker team as a result.

Did you have a strategy?

When we got down to the final three, we were just having a good time. None of us wanted anyone to go home at that point.

I didn't really have a strategy. It was just to have the ability to turn on the performance when you need to and not get involved in any of the drama. Getting involved in the drama can rattle your performance.

It all comes down to performance on the day. You see some of the best shooters in the world choke once or twice a season. I'm not different from that. Like everybody else, I'll shoot completely terribly one day and have a good performance the next. It all comes down to what happens on the day.

What was one of the most fun challenges?

The knife-throwing challenge was good. It took everybody outside of their comfort zone. Everyone in the competition was familiar with firearms, but having to use primitive weapons like that was a good thing. It's one thing the show does very well—it takes people out of their comfort zone and forces them into unusual situations where they have to adapt. You're on a balance beam and throwing over water. I'm surprised nobody fell in. I was looking forward to that.

My other favorite part was the finale with Chris Cerino. We got to shoot everything. Chris and I have become really good friends. We shoot together competitively. We stay in touch outside of the shooting sphere as well.

Shooting the fuse was challenging. We had to use a Beretta and shoot out a lit fuse before a charge exploded. I went first on shooting the fuse, so I had no idea of how fast that fuse would burn. So I made the mistake of shooting too close to the burning end of it and wound up having to chase it. The second time around, after I had screwed the pooch, I went to the opposite end of the fuse and just built a good group there and made sure I could cut it. If you went first, it was often a disadvantage.

Producers in the first season were learning on the fly. The program has really learned from its mistakes and improved in subsequent seasons. They changed things to make sure competitors would not see others compete to gain an advantage. They've been pushing the envelope more.

I came back to the show as an expert. We had a multigun challenge. We had lots of discussions with the producer on how to make that effective—to make it a good, fairly difficult challenge that would stretch all the competitors. I had input on the setup. I've been back for seasons two, three, and four. I introduced them to a bunch of old British guns in season four. I've done a little bit of consulting with the show, giving them feedback.

What did you learn from the show?

There were some guns there that I had never shot before, so it was good to have a brief introduction to them. You had a limited time to practice with them, and then you were thrown straight into the deep end. You have severely curtailed practice sessions with the experts, and I think that's a good thing. It stressed the adaptability of the competitor. In some instances, you would get as few as six or seven rounds to find the way the gun was shooting. We had great experts on hand to help us.

What was the most difficult part?

The most difficult thing was the lack of mental stimulation in the house. You couldn't be in contact with anyone outside the show. They set it up so there will be drama in the house and keep the whole thing bubbling.

Being in lockdown with sixteen people was an eye-opener—an interesting experience, to say the least. In the first season, there were eight or nine of us crammed into one room, which made for interesting evening conversations. It was like a giant frat house, minus the easy availability of alcohol and casual sex. You can quote me on that. There were only two occasions during the entire month's span where we could have a beer.

We had to come up with various inventive ways to amuse ourselves. One night, to cause some concern for the producers, we all hid in an extremely small cupboard under the stairs. We packed about ten people into this area about the size of your average garbage can. The producers were all looking for us.

Adam Benson was a notable prankster—we taped or lashed somebody into their bed at two o'clock in the morning. Chris Cerino is a little bit anal—so we'd run around the house putting picture frames at odd angles. We'd do a lot of childish stuff.

We'd play darts and hurl them from increasingly great distances. I think we went through about eight or nine sets of darts—most ending up in the neighbors' property.

Most of the drama was blown out of proportion. But all those guys [Bill and Kelly/Adam and Caleb] kissed and made up.

What advice would you give to young marksmen?

Shoot as much as you can. Try as wide a variety of guns as you can, and just have fun with it. Expose yourself to as many different shooting disciplines as you can. Figure which one you like the look of the best and, once you've decided that, talk to someone who has been in the shooting competitions. Shooters are normally very friendly guys, and they'll show you how to get started in the sport.

You'll never outgrow a good .22. They are very good training tools for when you go on to the bigger stuff, and they're very accurate and rewarding to shoot. Even if you get into the stratospheric realms of international competition, like Mike and J.J. in season one, you'll still never outgrow a good .22 pistol or rifle. If you're getting into firearms, that should be one of your first purchases.

You need to master the fundamentals of marksmanship before you begin acquiring a diversity of firearms. And the .22 is a great way to do that.

If you want to be on the show, eventually get as much exposure as you can to various different guns and nongun weapons. I didn't have any experience with a stick bow, but I hunted deer with a compound bow for years. I have never thrown a knife before.

How did you get started as a marksman?

I started at around age ten. My parents had a weekend place on a farm, and I wound up shooting with the farmer's son, who was about the same age as me. I shot his .22 rifle for the first time, and I never looked back after that. I got plenty of experience being in the British army.

I had my own machine shop. I was a woodworker for a lot of years. When I reached as far as I wanted in wood, I went into steel. I picked up enough skills to do some machining. There was crossover with that into firearms. So I wound up building a few guns for myself. A couple were my own designs. I was designing individual components to make a complete, whole firearm. I adapted a Russian submachine gun. If you're a shooter, you might wind up tinkering with guns and it just goes from there. These are one-offs for myself.

What are your plans from here?

I'd like to continue my career in the firearms industry and do more TV, getting in front of the camera. You just gotta be careful what you do in front of the cameras!

REMINGTON 700

COUNTRY: USA

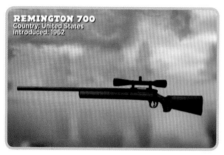

REMINGTON 700
Country: United States
Introduced: 1962

CALIBER: Varies from .17 to .308 (Winchester), and even .458

WEIGHT: Almost 9 pounds empty, without the telescope

BARREL LENGTH: Varies—20, 22, 24, and 26 inches

FEEDING SYSTEM: 3-, 4-, 5-, 6-round internal magazine

IN THE FIRST elimination challenge of season one, Kelly Bachand brought down Mike Seeklander in a competition with a scoped Remington 700 sniper rifle. Produced from 1962 through today, this is one of the most popular rifles worldwide because of its strength and reliability.

Based on a center-fire bolt action, the 700 fires a three-, four-, or five-round magazine, depending on the caliber. The weapon is often operated with a scope and bipod. The firearm comes in a broad range, with varying barrels, stocks, metal finishes, and calibers.

AR-15
(SEMIAUTOMATIC RIFLE)
COUNTRY: USA

AR-15
Country: United States
Introduced: 1958

CALIBER: .223 Remington, 5.56 NATO

WEIGHT: 5.5–8.5 pounds

BARREL LENGTH: Standard is 20 inches, but comes with adjustable lengths

FEEDING SYSTEM: Various STANAG magazines, detachable firearms magazines proposed by NATO—STANAG meaning Standardization (STAN) Agreement (AG)

THIS IS THE civilian derivative of the military M16 rifle, which came into service for jungle warfare in the early sixties and by 1969 was the standard rifle for the U.S. military. In episode four of season one, each player sees the grid for thirty seconds before it is covered up, then has twenty seconds to fire up to seven shots with the AR-15 and hit only the other team's targets. The small-arms firm ArmaLite first built the AR-15 and then sold the design to Colt.

A semiautomatic, gas-operated rifle constructed of aluminum alloys and synthetic materials, the gun is noted for its light weight, small caliber, accuracy, and high firing velocity. The fully automatic version can shoot eight hundred rounds per minute. It comes with collapsible stocks for shorter barrels and different hand guard configurations. *Top Shot* competitor Caleb Giddings called it "the LEGO system of weapons. You can do whatever you want to it."

KENTUCKY LONG RIFLE

COUNTRY: USA (ORIGINATED IN BRITAIN)

CALIBER: .60 (.36 and .45 also common)

WEIGHT: Variable

BARREL LENGTH: 35 inches

FEEDING SYSTEM: Muzzle-loaded

ALSO CALLED THE "American long rifle," the Kentucky long rifle played a crucial role in U.S. history. It was used in the American Revolution, the French and Indian War, and the War of 1812. In fact, the gun was crucial in the victory at the Battle of New Orleans in 1815.

The rifle got its name not from where it was made but because so many men from Kentucky used it. Historians say the gun was produced by German gunsmiths who had immigrated to Pennsylvania and Virginia as early as the 1620s. It was also the rifle of Daniel Boone, Davy Crockett, and other early frontiersmen. Many were at the Alamo. On the show *Antiques Roadshow*, an 1810 Kentucky long rifle was appraised at $20,000. In James Fenimore Cooper's *Last of the Mohicans*, Hawkeye carries a long rifle.

In episode five, the Red and Blue teams battle it out with a target-hitting contest using the Kentucky long rifle. Andre Robinson on the Red Team drills a shot almost into the center of the bull's-eye at fifty yards. Kelly hits the target at a hundred yards.

The first Kentucky long rifles were made "from a flat bar of soft iron, hand-forged into a gun barrel; laboriously bored and rifled with crude tools; fitted with a stock hewn from a maple tree in the neighboring forest, and supplied with a lock hammered to shape on the anvil." Those vivid words from John G. W. Dillon in 1924 venerably describe the rifle that helped our country win its independence in the late 1700s. The rifle fires with flintlock action from a single-action trigger-and-spring mechanism. The operation is simple. You have a piece of flint in the cock, you load powder and ball in the muzzle, and

you put powder in the pan. When you pull the trigger, the steel sets off a little spark, and the primary charge sets off the main charge—and the rifle fires. At the time it was described as light in weight, graceful in line, economical in consumption of powder and lead, and fatally precise. The very long barrel gives a good sighting plane and allows for an efficient use of powder. The instrument has an effective range of one hundred yards, but a master shooter can hit an apple from three hundred yards. Some versions of the gun feature elaborate decorative art.

WINCHESTER 73

COUNTRY: USA

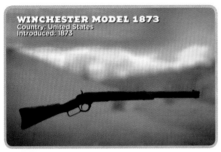

CALIBER: .44-40 (original caliber)

WEIGHT: 9.5 pounds

BARREL LENGTH: 49.3 inches

FEEDING SYSTEM: 15-round tube magazine

ALSO CALLED THE Winchester 1873, this is one of the most famous Winchester rifles ever. Like the Colt Peacemaker, it was dubbed a "Gun that Won the West" for the huge role it played with pioneers in the settling of the American frontier. Originally developed by the Winchester Repeating Arms Co., the first Winchester came out in 1866. And it has the title role in *Winchester '73*, an American Western made in 1950 starring Jimmy Stewart and Shelley Winters. In the spirit of the Wild West, contestants on season one had to use the Winchester to blast a bottle Annie Oakley–style—using a handheld mirror and shooting backward over their shoulder.

The 73 was steel-framed and originally chambered to shoot the powerful .44-40 cartridge but manufactured to fire .38-40 and .32-20. All Winchesters are called repeating rifles, because the lever mechanism allows a rifleman to get off several rounds without reloading; the shooter simply works the lever to reload fresh cartridges into the chamber of the barrel.

HK93
(HECKLER & KOCH RIFLE)
COUNTRY: GERMANY

CALIBER: .223 Remington

WEIGHT: About 8.4 pounds

BARREL LENGTH: 16.125 inches

FEEDING SYSTEM: From 5 to 40 rounds in a detachable box magazine

THIS WEAPON STARTED as a paramilitary-style weapon and became a semiautomatic sporting rifle. In the 1960s, Heckler & Koch developed the HK33, which in time led to the HK43 and HK93, which were introduced in 1974 and were weapons of choice of Western special forces. The HK93 is used in the season one elimination challenge, where contestants run uphill and stop at four shooting stations with one weapon and one target at each, shooting at ranges of 50, 100, 125, and 150 yards.

The HK93 semiautomatic rifle is an update of the HK43. It differs mainly in having a slightly shorter thread barrel that allows flash suppressors to be screwed on, thus reducing visual interference from burning gases that exit the muzzle.

GUN TALK

Sharpshooter

The name is synonymous with *marksman,* but the term doesn't come from the Sharps rifle. It originated in Austria at the turn of the eighteenth century.

SHARPS RIFLE

COUNTRY: USA

CALIBER: .52

WEIGHT: 9.5 pounds

BARREL LENGTH: (entire length) 47 inches (an inch short of 4 feet)

FEEDING SYSTEM: 1 round

AS SEASON TWO of *Top Shot* kicks off, Colby introduces all contestants to the Sharps rifle that was used 150 years ago by the Union Army when putting together its first sharpshooting regiment. To get in that elite group, marksmen had to pass a test, and on this first episode, *Top Shot* contestants face the exact same challenge: arcing lead downrange with the historic gun at a ten-inch target from two hundred yards. The two closest to the target—Jay Lim and Chris Reed—pick teams. The Sharps four-foot breech rifles were made famous in the Civil War by the Union's Berdan Sharpshooters. They were much more accurate than muzzle-loading muskets.

The Sharps series of rifles were designed by Christian Sharps, with his first being patented in 1848. The carbine version of the rifle was popular with both Confederate and Union armies for its shorter length, measuring in at thirty-nine inches compared to forty-seven inches. Both the rifle and the carbine were certainly an advantage over some of the six-foot-long muskets that were still in use at the time.

The Sharps is a single-shot weapon with an effective range of five hundred yards. It has a falling-block action. A shooter moves the solid metal breechblock vertically in grooves cut into the breech to load and unload. In the up position, the breechblock is locked and seals the chamber to fire. In the down position, the chamber opens to reload a cartridge from the rear. One of the selling points of the Sharps was that it held a stack of pelleted primers so the shooter didn't have to individually load each primer cap.

M1A

COUNTRY: USA

CALIBER: 7.62mm (Cartridge is a 7.62x51mm NATO)

BARREL LENGTH: 16–22 inches

WEIGHT: 7.8 to 11.6 pounds (empty magazine)

FEEDING SYSTEM: 20-round magazine. Also 5- and 10-round magazines

IN THE MILITARY-THEMED third episode of season two, competitors had to charge up a hill (or at least ascend it, as Maggie Reese recalls in her interview in the previous section) and blow up an ammo dump using the legendary M1A. Manufactured by the Springfield Armory starting in 1974, the M1A is the civilian version of the M14 rifle. During the 1960s, the M1A was known for reliability and simplicity. It is still used today as a sniper rifle, and some special operations units still use it. It was called the last of the battle rifles, because it was a heavy-duty, all-purpose infantry rifle.

This magazine-fed, gas-operated semiautomatic with a rotating bolt comes equipped with well-designed iron sights. The front is a blade sight and the rear is a circular peep sight. These sights are very accurate and help make the gun effective out to eight hundred meters.

Kentucky Long Rifle—Garry James
(Long Rifle Expert)

THE KENTUCKY LONG rifle was probably the first truly American firearm. This quintessentially American firearm descends from German and Swiss stock called Jaeger rifles. The way it works is a very simple flint-and-steel mechanism. What happens basically is you've got a piece of flint held in the cock. You have a little powder in the flash pan. When you cock the gun, the cock goes forward and strikes the flint against the steel. The steel makes sparks, and the sparks enter the pan. A charge inside the pan detonates the charge inside the barrel, which has already been muzzle-loaded with loose powder and a patched ball. I gave teams a little warning about watching the muzzle drop. Hang fires are a problem with any of these early types of ignition systems. The gun may not spark properly and may set off a charge. Wind can cause a little difficulty too. It's a long gun, so there can be a little bit of a problem with the direction of the wind.

Gas-operated

In a gas-operated firearm, a portion of high-pressure gas from the cartridge is used to power a mechanism that discharges the spent case and sets a new cartridge in the chamber.

RUGER 10/22 RIFLE

COUNTRY: USA

RUGER 10/22 RIFLE
Country: United States
Introduced: 1964

CALIBER: .22

WEIGHT: 5.25 pounds

BARREL LENGTH: 18.5 inches

FEEDING SYSTEM: 10- or 5-round rotary box magazine

STARTING PRODUCTION IN 1964, the 10/22 has enjoyed widespread popularity for the past forty-seven years, especially among small-game hunters and shooters looking for target practice and plinking. On episode eight of season two, the marksmen face off with the .22, a firearm that most were familiar with, taking out as many items as possible in a carnival-style shooting gallery featuring eighty targets—some moving (rotating ducks) and some stationary (jars with gumballs, little bottles, and big bottles).

Named for its ten-round magazine (although available in just the five-round form in many places) and chambered in a .22 long rifle cartridge, this semiautomatic, rimfired rifle features very low recoil and requires inexpensive ammunition. The rotary magazine fits flush with the bottom of the stock. A two-screw attachment system makes removal and replacement of the barrel easy.

M1 GARAND

COUNTRY: USA

CALIBER: .30

WEIGHT: 9.5 to 11.6 pounds

BARREL LENGTH: 24 inches

FEEDING SYSTEM: 8-round magazine

INTRODUCED IN 1936, the M1 Garand was the first semiautomatic rifle to be issued to the infantry of any nation. General George S. Patton dubbed the weapon "that greatest battle implement ever devised." The Garand replaced the 1903 Springfield as the standard-issue rifle of U.S. armed forces and was retired in 1957 in favor of the M14. Battle troops used the weapon in World War II, the Korean War, and to a limited extent in the Vietnam War. The semiautomatic firepower of the Garand gave the United States an advantage over the military forces of Germany, Italy, and Japan, who were usually armed with bolt-action rifles. The rifle is still a favorite among civilians for hunting, target shooting, and collecting. Drill teams and military honor guards also still employ the firearm.

This gas-operated rifle has an effective range of 440 yards. The weapon is fed ammo from a clip that is inserted from above into a fixed magazine. The clip system has been criticized for increasing the rifle's weight and complexity. Clips hold eight rounds of .30-06 Springfield ammunition. When it is expended, the rifle bolt automatically locks back and ejects the clip. Insert the clip and the bolt snaps forward, readying the gun to be fired.

Mike Hughes
Age: 38
Maple Falls, Washington
Season Three Finalist

MIKE IS PRESIDENT of the Firearms Training Equipment Company. He says that playing college football taught him more than attending engineering and law school. "Teamwork, preparation, execution," he explains. Nowadays, Mike draws on these ethics and his competitive spirit at the range. He's been participating in USPSA matches for the last ten years and recently earned a seventh-place title at the nationals. In 2009, after a decade of practicing law, Mike founded his own firearms-training company. He's even invented his own training pistol, which he calls the SIRT. When he isn't pistol training or running his company, Mike can be found lifting weights, sprinting, hiking, or spending time with his family. He describes himself as disciplined, but says he doesn't take himself too seriously. "I'm very competitive—I will win or die trying," he declares. "But I am always a good sport."

What was your favorite part of being on *Top Shot*?

One of my favorite challenges was the zip line challenge [traveling backward on a zip line twenty feet in the air at fifteen miles per hour, shooting targets with a Steyr Special Purpose Pistol]. That really taxed the fundamentals of shooting as far as sights and trigger control and transitioning, driving the gun, decelerating the gun, snapping the eyes—all those skill sets. The zip line felt so good.

I was really excited to get experience with the cannon—the Hotchkiss mountain gun. That's a once-in-a-lifetime. Shooting an AR, a 308 or the 15, is not a big deal, but shooting a cannon at $120 per round, that's a unique experience—just feeling the percussion from it.

Were there any particular strains of being on the show?

You have no external stimulus, so you have to socialize. You're cramming years into weeks, as far as creating human dynamics. You get on each other's nerves at an accelerated rate, which creates drama. And I get it. It's a necessary element and a lubricant for the main message of *Top Shot*, which for me is to promote firearms in a positive light.

The show is reality. It's real. But it's real in the same sense as a cockfight. A cockfight is real to the cocks, but it's an artificial, controlled environment. They are rubbing their heads together, putting razor blades on their feet. In some sense, I feel like that. We have psych exams; we all get profiled; we all get thrown in the mix. They agitate it up a little bit and let the cameras roll.

I think the biggest issue is the challenge of not going after anything. There's no daily objective, like when you go to work or when you train at home. Having nothing but showing up and competing for five minutes—being that clinically unproductive was mentally tough. One of my favorite lines from the movie *Heat* is from Pacino, and it applies here: "All I am is what I'm going after." And you have nothing to really go after all day.

You can work out, do some cardio, stretch out, lifting. And that might cover three hours. I felt good as far as the nutrition plan. Eating my protein—vegetables and stuff. You can journal. That's good for an hour or two maybe. You can listen to stories of others.

There's a philosophy behind competing. You have two brains on. You have your analytical self and your big dumb dog. The Zen comes out by being that big dumb dog. You're flowing. You're being in the zone. It's just Sport Science 101.

In my off time, I did a lot of visualizing. You just try to visualize every detail. Put different emphasis on things—how your feet feel, how your toes feel. For me, I visualize a lot of pistol craft, because that's where my love is.

[For instance,] the natural-point-of-aim drill for the blindfold competition with the trick shot was one of my favorite episodes. I did twenty training sessions from practice to the next day—short ones of three to fifteen minutes. Basically, I'd go out, walk in my triangle, open my eyes, and take a reference point off my hand.

I was working on natural point of aim. It worked out well. When you bring your arms up blindfolded you're naturally a few degrees lower than you think you are. It was a fun challenge I could practice for without having official practice.

What was it like being eliminated and then coming back to the show?

It helped to be out and get back in. When I got back in, I had a much better attitude—almost like a chemical change in my brain, because I didn't want to take it for granted. Before, I would get caught up in the minutiae. In the big picture, you're making a show and it's going to touch a lot of people. When you have a chance to reparticipate, you get recalibrated into the bigger picture, the bigger message, the bigger meaning. My attitude was so much better, and that made my performance better to make it to the finals. Even something way outside my comfort zone just felt fun.

You got to love what you're doing. It put me in that good state of being relaxed but having a lot of intensity behind it. There was a real spot there. If you're not having fun with it, you get pulled into a zone where you have tightness. Dustin [winner of season three] took the whole competition as a relaxed thing. He took it one day at a time, and in the end he never had any deficiencies that caused him to falter.

What are some tips you have for new marksmen?

It comes down to quality training. It has to be in high volume while ensuring quality of movement. I would strongly advocate emphasis on the fundamentals. In shooting, it's grip, stance, sight alignment, sight picture, shooter control, breathing, and follow-through. Breathing is a fundamental for marksmen. In an environment where there is a heavy accuracy component, it's really understanding the timing of breathing and when are optimal times to pull a trigger. When you take a shot you settle in, clear the chest cavity, and pull the trigger. Breathing is a fundamental. It's apparent that we're modifying our breaths to synchronize with our movements to get a better performance.

I think too many people get focused on whiz-bang peripheral issues instead of zeroing in and focusing on those fundamentals.

Keep an open mind and absorb as much different information from different sources so you can get better. Don't sit on a false peak somewhere and think you're the biggest/baddest—you got to jump out of your comfort zone, basically.

Life begins at the edge of your comfort zone. All too often we get in our own drills, our own social structure, our own range, with its own setup and apparatuses, and we feel like we're badasses. Look in that ugly mirror. Don't make excuses for it. Don't demonize it.

Are you ever recognized?

It's amazing how many people will stop you and talk about the show—particularly at airports. I'll tell you what's really positive about the show is that a lot of the people I interface with are not even shooters. And that's one of the reasons I really like *Top Shot*. I like the show because it promotes firearms in a positive way. It exposes marksmanship and safe usage in creative ways. And social drama is a lubricant to keep it a complete show, so it's not a real sterile competition.

How has your life changed because of the show?

It helps my business in terms of making relationships. If I talk to some other person—a vendor or someone—they can identify with me because they've seen me.

What's next for you?

I'm set up now to get involved with three-gun competitions, which is rifle, pistol, shotgun, and a winter Bullseye league. After the series ended, I was in USPSA nationals. I slipped this year to fifteenth. I didn't perform as well this year as I would have liked. I was seventh last year. My goal as a marksman is to win USPSA nationals. Business is going huge. My trinity is work, family, training.

FAL
COUNTRY: BELGIUM

FAL
Country: Belgium
Introduced: 1951

CALIBER: .30 and 7.62x51mm NATO cartridge

WEIGHT: 8.4 to 13.1 pounds

BARREL LENGTH: 21 inches

FEEDING SYSTEM: 20- to 30-round detachable box magazine

IN SEASON TWO, Iain Harrison, the Top Shot of season one, returns to lead the remaining six contestants into a four-gun challenge, shooting from an unsteady platform. One of the rifles that Iain chooses is the FAL, or the Fusil Automatique Léger (light automatic rifle). Designed between 1947 and 1953, the gun became one of the most famous and widespread rifle designs. Many North Atlantic Treaty Organization (NATO) nations adopted it during the Cold War, with the exception of the United States. Manufactured by Fabrique Nationale de Herstal, or FN for short, the rifle was widely used globally during the Cold War, earning the nickname "right arm of the Free World."

This gas-operated semiautomatic can blast six to seven hundred rounds per minute. It uses a tilting breechblock locking mechanism. The World Guns Web site describes the action as follows: "After the shot is fired, the gas piston makes a quick tap to the bolt carrier and then returns back, and the rest of the reloading cycle is commenced by the inertia of bolt group."

BENELLI M2 SUPER 90 SHOTGUN

COUNTRY: ITALY

CALIBER: 12- or 20-gauge

WEIGHT: 7 to 8 pounds

BARREL LENGTH: 20 inches (also 18.5 and 14 inches)

FEEDING SYSTEM: 3- to 7-round tubular magazine

INTRODUCED IN 2005, the Benelli M2 Super 90 is a semiautomatic shotgun available in different versions for civilian, military, and law enforcement use. Chris Reed and Jamie Franks go head-to-head in an elimination using the tricked-out modern shotgun toward the end of season two. Made by Benelli Armi Spa, the firearm is known for easy maintenance and reliability.

The standard-model Benelli offers a lightweight aluminum-alloy receiver and tubular magazine. Instead of the traditional gas-cycling operation, the M2 Super 90 features an inertia-driven recoil system. This is the newest design in recoil-operated firearms, using almost the whole weapon as the recoiling component while the bolt remains stationary during firing. The gun can be fitted with traditional iron sights or ghost-ring diopter sights. Ghost-ring sights have a fast aperture and obscure a target less than most other sights, and they are often used on combat shotguns. Laser pointers and tactical flashlights can also be mounted on the Benelli.

GUN TALK

Receiver

The section of the gun that contains the trigger and most of the moving parts.

AK 47

COUNTRY: FORMER SOVIET UNION

CALIBER: 7.62x39mm cartridge

WEIGHT: 11.5 pounds with a loaded magazine

BARREL LENGTH: 16.3 inches

FEEDING SYSTEM: 10-, 20-, 30-, 40-, 75-, or 100-round detachable box and drum-style magazine. The rifle is also compatible with the 40-round box or 75-round drum magazine from the RPK Soviet machine gun.

SHORT FOR AVTOMAT Kalashnikova, the AK is an assault rifle that began development at the very end of World War II and was introduced in official Soviet military trials in 1946. By 1947, select units of the Soviet army began using the weapon, and in 1949, it was an official weapon of all Soviet armed forces. The rifle is widely used to this day, because it is relatively inexpensive, long-lasting, and easy to use. Critics have said that the gun's ruggedness and reliability come at the price of accuracy. Down to the final three in season three, Mike Hughes challenges his other two competitors with an unprecedented shot—firing at whiskey bottles at one hundred feet with the AK 47, using their strong hand only—unsupported. While Mike thinks he might gain an advantage with the shot, Dustin Ellermann and Gary Quesenberry are both able to match Mike in this competition.

This gas-operated assault rifle is a selective-fire weapon; it has at least one semiautomatic and one automatic mode. One of its innovations is an underfolding metal shoulder stock. It is capable of blasting six hundred rounds per minute.

LARUE TACTICAL OBR (OPTIMIZED BATTLE RIFLE)
COUNTRY: USA

CALIBER: 7.62 NATO

WEIGHT: 9 pounds, 11 ounces

BARREL LENGTH: 18 inches, although 16.1- and 20-inch variables are available

FEEDING SYSTEM: 20-round magazine (or 10-round)

IN EPISODE SIX of season three, marksmen compete with this recently released, ultramodern assault rifle. Constructed by Austin Precision Products, the LaRue Tactical line of weapons is used among military and law enforcement personnel as well as professional shooting competitors. With the OBR, a modified high-capacity magazine makes it a smooth feed compared to previous similar rifles. The weapon costs close to $3,000.

This is a 7.62 NATO lightweight sniper-grade rifle based on a 5.56 NATO platform, and uses a direct-gas-impingement system. A SureFire muzzle device tames flash. It has no sights but a rail for mounting optics.

Jay Lim

Placentia, California
Occupation: Golf Instructor
Season Two

"**I'M NOT JUST** a shooter; I'm an athlete. I'm a thinker. I'm all that. Whatever I think—I can get my body to do." Jay Lim is an amateur shooter, and he has competed in archery events on a national level, once making it all the way to the 2004 Olympic trials. And he doesn't excel at just archery—he also competes with the air pistol, air rifle, at skeet, and with handguns. He's a self-described overachiever who loves marksmanship because "there is perfection in shooting, and that is what I strive for."

What did you enjoy?

Shooting the thousand-yard shot was fun. That was an iconic rifle, the Barrett .50 cal. It's banned in California. I couldn't buy one of those if I wanted to. Even that bullet is $15 per shot, so chances of me being able to shoot that gun were very low. On the show, they just said, "Keep firing until you hit the target."

Did anything particularly bother you in the experience?

I was criticized for not taking the expert advice. The thing is, I did take their advice. We did try it their way, and my way was better. I am a sports instructor myself. If I went to a tournament and one of the golfers said, "What can I do with my swing right now? I'm going to compete this afternoon." I'd say, "You have to do it the way you've practiced it. Because if I give you something now, you're going to be doing something on the course that you've never done before." And that's what they were asking me to do. "Hey, go out there and do your best doing something that you've never done before." That doesn't make sense to me.

If they were going to vote me up for elimination not based on my shooting but based on how close your relationship is with the other people, that's not a shooting show. I went on the show to shoot. I didn't go on the show to make friends, even though I did. It doesn't become a shooting show at that point. Shooting is objective, not subjective. "Did I hit the target or not? Did I do it in enough time or not?"

Do you stay in touch with former contestants?

Daryl and I got along the best. And I keep in contact with him the most now. Once in a while I will shoot with Kyle. He's fifteen minutes away from me. I beat Daryl in an elimination, but he and I are the closest. It was a great opportunity to shoot against a trained military shooter. That guy has got medals; he's a decorated shooter.

What was the hardest part of being on the show?

No contact with my family. No books, no TV. All I wanted to know was that my family was okay. But I couldn't contact them unless there was an emergency.

Living with the other guys was fine. We all got along and I was treated well. And I treated everyone else with the same amount of respect and courtesy. Our season we had meals all together all the time, and there was never a question of who was going to cook and who was going to wash. Everyone always helped. I think something unique about our season was that everyone got along really well.

What would people like to know about behind the scenes?

There were many story lines they could have shown. When I watched season one, Brad came across as a total complainer, but when I met him in Vegas at the 2010 SHOT show, he was a great guy. We spent a day shooting, and he went to dinner with my family.

There are people out there who may think I'm a jerk, but I'm one of the nicest guys you'll meet.

To keep ourselves amused, we made weapons. Chris Reed made a blowgun out of a curtain rod. We were throwing steak knives at the dartboard. We had a deck of cards—that was pretty much it.

Your season had a lot of physical challenges—dodging paintballs and running up a hill to shoot those ammo dumps. How was the physical challenge of it all?

Growing up I ran track and field. I was a high jumper. I was a long jumper and a triple jumper. I ran in high school and college. So this wasn't a problem.

You picked teams by really looking at their backgrounds, and Chris seemed to pick teams more based on his gut. What do you think about how that worked out?

I like to do the homework. I got on the show and didn't know anybody. So how was I going to pick my team without knowing what anybody does? You could call it an interview process, but how else was I supposed to pick a team if I didn't know how they shoot?

What have you noticed has changed since you were on the show?

One of the things about being a fan of the History Channel—it is a great experience to watch myself on a channel that I watch. Kind of surreal to turn on the TV and see the commercial and you see yourself on there. You can't even pay for that.

A lot of people recognized me after I was on the show. There were three million people watching the premiere show of our season. As far as going out there—if you go to a shooting range, someone is going to recognize you. It's died down at other places. I like it. For me the more people who know about me, the better my business does.

What are you currently doing?

I'm currently a golf instructor. One of the things I pride myself on is that I'm one of the leading authorities on golf biomechanics. I'm creating an interactive golf-training software.

I have taught both golf and how to shoot, and I can tell you that good golfers make great shooters, but the reverse is not always true—because good golfers need coordination and multiple body parts at different times. Shooting is pretty easy, to line up sights and pull the trigger. In golf, it's kind of like dancing and ballet and karate—you have to be really accurate, because all those motions wind up in one true moment, which is impact. If you swing wrong and hit the ball wrong by a quarter of an inch, you're done. That's why in golf, there's no par one. But there is perfection in shooting, because it's possible.

Did you grow from being on *Top Shot*?

Absolutely. In business, you want to be known. One of my biggest fears was, *What if I get myself out there and show people who and what I am, and they don't like me?* That was a huge fear, and that was holding me back from being the famous golf instructor that I was hired to be. The show put me out there, and I had to deal with people who didn't like me. Some outwardly criticized and ridiculed and publicly showed their dislike. The big lesson came from Adam Benson (season one). He called me and said, "Hey, look—I just saw what happened on the show, and this is what you got to know. There're as many people who don't like you as who do like you. And eventually, if you are a good person, the truth will come out." And sure enough, from the fourth episode on, people were rooting for me. And now I'm okay putting myself out there, putting my theories out there, putting my book out there— *Single Digit Handicap in 13 Weeks*. Now I understand. Put yourself out there. If you're good at what you do, and you're a good person and have the right motives, the truth will come out. I'm not afraid to put myself out there. There are people who like me and people who don't like me. Adam gave me valuable advice.

HEAVY
ARTILLERY

SOME OF THE most dramatic moments on *Top Shot* have come when marksmen blasted the heavy artillery—the Thompson .45 submachine gun, the Bulldog Gatling gun, the Hotchkiss mountain gun, and the grenade launcher. These are weapons that fire either rapid rounds or larger-caliber ammunition, or both. But being a top marksman means knowing how to take out a target, no matter the size of the weapon. That was shown on the *Top Shot* episode that began with players using the oldest-known weapon—the rock, to pick off tin cans—and ended with an elimination challenge using the Hotchkiss to hurtle two-pound projectiles more than a mile downrange.

As Colby, Mike Hughes, and many of the shooters can tell you, marksmanship comes down to the same fundamentals no matter what the weapon. You have to be able to aim, get targets in your sights, set the angle of fire, account for factors like wind and projectile drop as it travels, and fire the weapon without doing the equivalent of jerking the trigger. It always comes down to keeping the weapon steady and firing on course.

For the contestants on *Top Shot* who had the opportunity, this was a once-in-a-lifetime chance. Some of the guns, like the bag gun and Hotchkiss, are so rare that contestants would be unlikely to ever have the chance to use them outside of the show. Even if they did, the cost of the ammunition can be very expensive (there's no dry-firing a cannon). A big sniper rifle, like the .50-caliber Barrett, costs $15 a round. High-explosive 40mm grenades run $400 to $500 per cartridge. Plus, safe spaces to fire a big weapon like a cannon are hard to come by. The makers of the reality show *Mythbusters* found that out the hard way when they lobbed a cannonball from a bomb range in the hills near a suburban San Francisco Bay neighborhood. The ball entered the front door of a home and traveled through its master bedroom before landing on a neighbor's parked minivan. Talk about a loose cannon. Luckily the home was empty and no one was hurt.

Military personnel are the most likely to have experience with heavy artillery. Cannons and similar big weapons have been crucial to winning many military battles as far back as the latter 900s, during the Song Dynasty in China, when projectile-fire cannons were being developed. Cannons were fired during battles in the Middle Ages, including the Hundred Years' War in the fourteenth century. As time went on, cannons became lighter and more mobile. Gustavus Adolphus of Sweden demonstrated the value of an agile cannon. Outnumbered by Dutch forces in 1631, Adolphus relied on firing many volleys from cannons to win the battle. He also pioneered the canister shot, which was basically a can filled with musket balls. By the seventeenth century, English ships were lined with cannons, and sea battles were waged using this heavy artillery. In the early 1800s, weapons developers focused on making cannons more accurate, and enhanced their long-range capabilities. Napoleon Bonaparte depended on cannons for his rise to power in 1804, and he made savvy tactical use of the weapon in fighting the Russians and British before being defeated at the Battle of Waterloo in 1815. In the twentieth century, cannons grew in power and sophistication. Superheavy howitzers could propel shells high in the air, giving them a steep angle of descent that could enable strikes in "protected" areas. In World War I, the Germans relied on their howitzer, nicknamed Big Bertha, and Britain had its fifteen-inch howitzer. In warfare today, the United States uses an M198 howitzer with a range of fourteen miles; it blasts a 155mm (6.1-inch) shell.

Those who made it the farthest on *Top Shot* enjoyed the opportunity to shoot the big guns, and embraced the marksmanship skills required to fire them with accuracy, showing again that fundamentals always matter.

"Timber" Challenge: SEASON THREE

THE SETUP: In practice, Mark Schneider and Michael Marelli take turns shooting 120 rounds each at three separate stripes on a board, under the guidance of expert Garry James. "Competitors need to be smart about the time it takes to reload," says James. Strategic shooting as opposed to spraying the target is the more successful way to go. In practice, both competitors have to learn how to adjust the gun on its tripod, manipulating different dials, to take aim. "This is like the steampunk of machine guns," says Michael. "It takes so many movements to aim. Shooting the Gatling is definitely like rubbing your head and patting your stomach at the same time." In a side-by-side challenge, Mark and Michael have to cut completely through three wooden telegraph posts. Each post is four inches wide, and they are set

at fifteen, twenty, and twenty-five yards. The marksman who does it first wins and avoids elimination.

The Bulldog Gatling gun is more compact than its predecessors, but designed to be operated by an experienced two-man team—one who loads and one who fires. With this teamwork, the Gatling could fire a thousand rounds per minute, or fifteen a second. The twist for *Top Shot* competitors is that each would have to shoot the gun on his own with no help.

THE OUTCOME: Michael cuts the first pole down first. Mark is hitting low and can't see his bullet holes in the wood. He is having a hard time seeing the hits. But they both down the second poles in unison. Michael's Gatling starts to move around, and he has to hold it steady with his hand. Both men pound away at the final target.

THE ELIMINATION CHALLENGE: Michael mows through all three of his telegraph polls first, and Mark is eliminated. "There're thousands of people who try out for this competition and never get selected," says Mark. "I did. I'm pretty happy about that. Today, we got to see a historic weapon come to life. Done in by a Gatling gun. Never would have thunk it."

1877 BULLDOG GATLING GUN

COUNTRY: USA

CALIBER: .45-70 government cartridge

WEIGHT: 135 pounds, and another 135 pounds for the tripod mount

BARREL LENGTH: Five 18.25-inch barrels

FEEDING SYSTEM: Wooden loading blocks capable of holding 20 rounds each

ON EPISODE FOUR of season three, *Top Shot* brought out one of its biggest guns to date with the Gatling gun. Marksmen had to split four-inch-wide wood poles set at fifteen, twenty, and twenty-five yards. Created in 1861 by Dr. Richard J. Gatling, a dentist by profession, this weapon is one of the earliest rapid-fire firearms, and a forerunner of the machine gun. Although it is called the first weapon of mass destruction, Gatling thought the weapon would enable armies to be

smaller, and so decrease the number of deaths ultimately caused by war. Union forces used the Gatling toward the end of the American Civil War, and it played a crucial role in the Spanish-American War during the decisive and bloody Battle of San Juan Hill in 1898.

The original Gatling relied on six barrels rotating around a central shaft, powered by a hand crank. (Some models have ten barrels.) The biggest innovation was a gravity-feed system that allowed relatively unskilled shooters to easily load and fire at a rate of about two hundred rounds per minute. With later models the rate increased to twelve hundred rounds per minute. More compact and easier to use than its predecessors, the five-barrel 1877 Bulldog model used on *Top Shot* could fire about one thousand rounds per minute when operated by an experienced two-man team loading and cranking the weapon. The shells drop into the breech from a hopper or stick magazine at the top of the gun, and an independent firing mechanism activates as the shooter cranks. The weapon possesses surprising accuracy with a tight spray pattern.

CONTESTANT Q&A

Gary Quesenberry
Job: Agent for Homeland Security
Hometown: Cleveland, Ohio
Age: 40

GARY SERVED IN the U.S. Army during Operation Desert Storm and was a member of the Special Operations Response Team for the Federal Bureau of Prisons. He completed the Triple Nickel Course of Fire and owns a Triple Nickel, along with fellow Homeland Security agent Jarrett Grimes. At home, he has a wife and three children.

How did you get into shooting?

I grew up in a little town in Virginia in the Appalachian Mountains, right on the border of North Carolina. Shooting and marksmanship in general are a big part of life down there, not so much as a hobby but out of necessity. My parents and my grandparents all grew up shooting. It was something I was always exposed to. I was somewhat of a hunter. My dad had a huge influence on teaching me about marksmanship and weapon safety, and kind of took the mystery out of things. I think that's a big problem nowadays. Kids are fascinated with guns because they hold a lot of mystery to them. That's why they're drawn to them. But if you take the mystery out of it, it all boils down to that it's just a tool. And it's a tool that I became very proficient with at a very early age. Before I could hold a rifle on my own, my dad would hold one up for me, and talk me through sighting, and let me pull the trigger on it. Once I got older, he put the gun on my shoulder, and he would hold it up because I wasn't strong enough to hold it by myself. He let me get used to the recoil and noise and walked me through things so I was never scared of a gun.

I grew up with three brothers, and we were all very competitive, and one of the things we were always competitive in was marksmanship. It's something that is highly prized where I come from. We didn't deal just with guns. You set up a bunch of cans on a fence post and try to knock them off with rocks. Very similar to what you saw in the competition. It was something that we were always doing. In the absence of PlayStation 3s, we got rocks and cans. It was always a lot of fun.

I've never been a really big competition shooter. I turned seventeen and I joined the army, and they put the finishing touches on my marksmanship skills—the foundation that my father laid for me. Once I got out of the army, I started working for the government. I was part of a special operations response team, on which you deal with several different types of weapons. I became an agent for the Department of Homeland Security. It seemed like my career path in marksmanship had been laid at a very early age.

Which competitions did you especially enjoy?

I enjoyed every one of them. The one that sticks out the most for me is the very second competition that we had with the AK 47. There was an obstacle course involved. It was a freezing cold day. It was wet, muddy, and miserable conditions, and for us to pull off a win under those conditions was very satisfying for us as a team. We had the mud pit, exploding mortars, waist-deep freezing-cold water. I think it did a lot to gel us together as a team. Because at that point we had been labeled the losers. I was on the Red Team. The way they broke the teams up in the beginning was to shoot the Smith & Wesson 500; losers go to this bench, winners go to this bench. Colby even referred to us as the losing team. We learned pretty quickly that if you can't pull yourself together under conditions like those, you are pretty much going to flounder as a team for the rest of the competition. It really made me happy that we pulled that one off, because it really made us more cohesive as a team.

One thing that I learned very early on is, You may be very well-prepared to shoot whatever firearm they throw at you, but you're probably not prepared to shoot that firearm under the conditions you're going to shoot it under. I may be able to shoot an H&K machine pistol, but I probably never practiced shooting while spinning around on a one-armed Ferris wheel at fifteen miles per hour.

Those are the types of things that level the playing field, and if you can pull yourself together under those types of circumstances, then you know you have a winning group.

What weapons were you glad you had an opportunity to use?

I really enjoyed the archery challenge, because I used to really enjoy archery when I was younger. And that challenge really did a lot to reestablish that connection. Once I won my Bass Pro Shop card against Mike Hughes, once I got home, I went straight out and bought a Martin X-200 recurve bow. I really started working on my archery skills and that instinctive shooting—there's no bells and whistles; it's just you and your talent. It's rewarding to be able to practice with something like that and see the progress and improvement. So archery was a particular favorite of mine. We were shooting off a ramp and into a moving target.

The weapons I didn't do so well with, like the McMillan TAC-50 . . . I completely blew that challenge. I was the worst by far and I just couldn't get it right. And I realized that that was a sticking point for me. That was something I had to work on. I've done a lot of work since I left there to improve that, because whether you enjoy the weapons system or not, you can learn something about yourself no matter what you're doing.

With the McMillan TAC-50, we were shooting at a target five hundred yards away. It's moving back and forth. You start in a standing position, and when Colby said go you had to drop down, load the weapon, and take a shot. Almost everybody did it in one or two shots. It took me fourteen shots.

I can tell you exactly what the problem was—we had a lot of very analytical people on season three. Jake, Mike Hughes, and Alex—these guys, when we were out there doing the practice, they get these notebooks out and they write down all the numbers and equations: "The bullet comes out at such a velocity, and if the targets are moving at so many miles per hour from the left to the right, how does that affect the impact of the bullet?" And then you take into consideration the wind—if it's blowing left to right and what speed. How do you gauge it? And they're taking all these notes. So that night, in the house, they're sitting down and figuring out all these equations that they need to know. And I'm kind of walking around the house with a bowl of Cheerios, poking fun at them a little bit. As soon as I lay down with that gun, there were sixty-five-mile-per-hour gusts of wind. And that affects the way the bullet travels. And when I lay down, I started all of a sudden getting all these numbers flipping around in my head—like the velocity and the movement of the target and the wind. I kind of panicked. I locked up. I didn't know where I should be holding my crosshairs or what adjustments I should be making to the scope, because I didn't do my homework. That's where I had the biggest problem.

If there's one message I'd like to put out there based on my performance in that challenge, it would be for the kids in math class [who say], "When am I ever going to use this again?" You may find yourself in need of that at some point, and you may look foolish if you don't know what you're doing.

Tell me about Dustin.

I never saw Dustin nervous. Watching Dustin during the *Top Shot* competition was like watching a kid at a carnival. He was there to have fun. There was no thought as to what would happen if he didn't perform well. He was relaxed to the point where he didn't get stressed, and it showed in his performance.

What other weapons did you enjoy using?

I really enjoyed the LaRue Optimized Battle Rifle in the first challenge. That was a really great gun to shoot. It was really smooth and fluid, and it doesn't have any of the recoil that you'd expect a .308 to have. It really is a cutting-edge weapon, but I think the most fun weapon for me to shoot was the one that we shot every time we went to the elimination range—that was the single-action Colt Peacemaker. It was one of the most historic guns that we shot, but very little was covered about it. When you think about it, the Colt Peace-maker was the gun that won the West. That gun played a huge part in our culture as Americans.

My whole life I've shot a lot of guns, but shooting basically comes down to three things: sight management, trigger control, and follow-through. It doesn't matter what you're shooting. Those three things are always there. Mike was so familiar with one particular weapons system that he was slow to adapt to anything new. When he ran into a problem with that weapons system that we had in the challenge, it slowed him down. Whenever he slowed down, that put me ahead a little bit and gave me the advantage. It was a tough win. Don't get me wrong: Mike Hughes is one hell of a shot, and he's tough to compete against, but it's that little difference in adaptability that won me the challenge.

Did you have a strategy when you made it to the final three?

When you're in the final three, you know you have one episode left, and *Top Shot* has followed a pattern. The big final challenge at the end has every weapon you've fired to that point set out. I knew in the final three that the only person who was going to beat me was going to be me. If I lost it was going to be because I let the competition get into my head.

What did you learn from being on the show?

You learn a lot. One thing is, you learn how you react with other people under stressful situations. I like to think of myself as a levelheaded guy, but being able to maintain that under the amount of stress that you're under for the entire competition is a challenge, and it says a lot about you as a person. Jake was the wild card.

What did you do to stay occupied during the downtime?

We played so much chess it was ridiculous. We had dice. We came up with these dice games. Jarrett and I kept dice in our pocket, so whenever we had downtime, we'd be throwing craps in the dirt out there on the range. We played a lot of card games. When Jarrett left, Phil built the Jarrett Grimes memorial craps table out of one of the drawers from one of the desks. Jake came up with extreme bocce ball that we'd play out in the yard until we started to break a few lights and windows. In extreme bocce, when you're playing by Jake's rules, the entire yard is fair game. We would throw the target ball into flower beds and up against the side of the house, which would lead to problems. It was a lot of fun, but it caused a lot of nightmares for the production staff.

After every third episode, which is basically nine days, you have a dark day. They bring in a TV and a couple of DVDs and the mics are off and the cameras are off and you get to let your hair down. That's when you get to see the real people who are there with you, when you know the cameras aren't in your face. One of the things we did too, that they didn't show on our season, was that every night when the sun started going down, there were beautiful sunsets there. We'd all go outside and sit on the patio and watch the sun go down. That was like our regularly scheduled programming. In the absence of all the other things you usually have in your life—the e-mails, the phone calls, and the televisions—this was something that became most important. You actually leave there with an appreciation of the smaller things.

Do you stay in touch with the other competitors?

Of course, Jarrett Grimes and I stay in touch. I talk to a lot of guys on the show. I still get regular phone calls from Chris Collins. I've spoken with Mike Hughes and Phil. You take friendships away from there that you'll maintain the rest of your life.

What advice do you have for beginning marksmen?

The important thing is that you don't go into this with any bad habits; you want to make sure you're always reinforcing good habits when you're first learning to shoot. The first step in that is finding somebody who is good at what you're into, whether it's archery or rifle shooting or pistol shooting. You have to find somebody who is not only good at it, but knows how to teach it. Some people are fantastic shots, but they don't know how to tell you why they're a fantastic shot. Everything boils down to a few fundamentals, and if you can master those, you'll always be good at what you do, and you reinforce that through practice. A good friend of mine said that repetition is the mother of all skills. So once you hone the fundamentals, repetition is the key.

The Hotchkiss Mountain Gun, the Gatling Gun, and the Spanish-American War 1898 3.2-inch Bag Gun

The Spanish-American War was a short-lived ten-week conflict between the United States and Spain, lasting from April 25 to August 12, 1898. Cubans had been revolting against Spanish rule for decades prior to the war. As news of Spanish atrocities in Cuba reached America, the public outcry for U.S. involvement swelled. The sinking of the American battleship *Maine* under mysterious circumstances in Havana Harbor amped up pressures for the United States to take action. To lose Cuba would be economically disastrous for Spain. The war was not just waged in Cuba, as the United States extended the battle-front to the Philippines and Guam in the Pacific and to Puerto Rico in the Caribbean. Big cannons like the Hotchkiss, the Gatling gun, and the bag gun played a decisive role in the United States winning the war. Cuba gained its independence, and the U.S. annexed Puerto Rico, the Philippines, and Guam.

Submachine Gun

Combines the automatic fire of a machine gun with the cartridge of a pistol. The submachine gun fires the pistol cartridge (such as a 9mm), while the machine gun fires either a full-size or intermediate-size round (such as a 7.62mm) typically used in a main battle or assault rifle. A submachine gun houses its ammunition, whereas a machine gun feeds from a belt. A submachine gun is much lighter than a machine gun and can be operated by one person, while a machine gun ordinarily takes two people to operate.

THOMPSON .45 SUBMACHINE GUN
("TOMMY GUN")

COUNTRY: USA

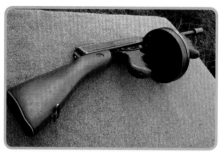

CALIBER: .45 ACP (Automatic Colt Pistol) cartridge

WEIGHT: 10.6 to 10.8 pounds

BARREL LENGTH: 10.5 inches

FEEDING SYSTEM: 50-round magazine (also 20- and 30-round magazines)

ON THE SECOND episode of season two's *Top Shot*, tiny Athena Lee (she's about five feet tall) blasted this iconic machine gun, only to be defeated by Jamie Franks. Franks and Lee shot through a porthole in a door at a red line on an eight-inch-wide board, trying to split it from twenty-five feet. General John T. Thompson invented the "tommy gun" in 1919, and it gained notoriety with Prohibition-era criminal and law enforcement agents. Hollywood popularized the gun in films, often showing skirmishes with gangsters firing from moving automobiles. Some criminals would hide the weapon in a violin case to carry it undetected. One writer labeled it "the gun that made the twenties roar." The weapon earned several slang names, including "Chicago Typewriter," "Chicago Piano," "Trench Sweeper," and "the Chopper." Thompson envisioned the weapon for military use to "sweep" troops from the trenches. Soldiers in World War II, the Greek Civil War, and the Korean War fought using the Thompson.

This powerful gun fires six hundred to fifteen hundred rounds per minute, but compared to modern 9mm machine guns, the weapon is heavy. Its weight, combined with a heavy trigger pull, makes it easy for a shooter to drift off target. Most people may picture the gun with its original drum magazine, but this was replaced with a more convenient box magazine.

EXPERT VIEW

Hotchkiss Mountain Gun— Rick Pohlers
(Cannon Enthusiast and Spanish-American War Reenactor)

OPERATING THE HOTCHKISS is an involved process. Competitors have to know how to open the breech, how to extract the expended case, how to clean the barrel, how to load a round, how to sight the target, and how to stand to the side and fire. The gun has an extremely powerful recoil and rolls back a few feet after each shot. So the shooter must also roll the cannon back into position after each shot, as well as take maybe thirty seconds or so to swab out the barrel to clean the residue. The buildup will affect the consistency of shot placement. Additionally, the gun gives off a tremendous amount

of smoke, and, depending on the wind, that will affect how well a shooter can see where his shot hits, which can make it tough to adjust and make corrections. Shooters need to use Kentucky windage, or adjust the aiming point and the elevating mechanism that controls the angle of the cannon barrel.

HOTCHKISS MOUNTAIN GUN

COUNTRY: FRANCE

CALIBER: 1.65" shells
WEIGHT: 121 pounds
LENGTH OF TUBE: 3.83 feet
LENGTH OF BORE: 3.43 feet
FEEDING SYSTEM: Breech-loaded

IN 1876, BENJAMIN Hotchkiss and his French firm, Hotchkiss Ordnance Company, introduced a portable cannon designed to be mounted on a light carriage and travel easily with cavalry or army troops moving through rough terrain. The gun and its accessories could be loaded onto two mules. It replaced the heavier twelve-pound mountain howitzer. Over twenty years, the United States bought about fifty-six of these cannons and used them in combat against the Nez Perce Indians and during the Spanish-American War and in the Philippines. It was used to devastating effect at the battles of San Juan Hill and Wounded Knee. They were designed for four-man teams—a loader, an aimer and shooter, a gun commander (to spot where it hit), and someone to take care of ammunition. On the season three *Top Shot* challenge, Mike Hughes dominated over Jarrett Grimes, bombing three water towers from 180 to 220 yards.

Well-built and simple to operate, the quick-firing, breech-loaded Hotchkiss was constructed of steel and relied on destructive shells—either common shells that would explode on impact and shower enemies with jagged shell fragments or canisters that would spray a fan-shaped pattern of half-inch hardened lead balls. On *Top Shot*, marksmen fired a two-pound projectile made of solid zinc. The Hotchkiss has a range in excess of thirty-five hundred yards and can fire a projectile at thirteen hundred feet per second. The spin given to the projectile increases its accuracy. The gun was the first to fire a self-contained round, meaning the cartridge contained the powder as well as the projectile. It has great power and rolls back after firing. Lanyards are long, so shooters can step out of the way of the recoil. The Hotchkiss is aimed not unlike a rifle, but it is loud and produces a lot of smoke and flame.

CONTESTANT Q&A

Dustin Ellermann
Age: 28
Zavalla, Texas

DUSTIN ELLERMANN WAS season three's Top Shot. Coming into the competition as a young summer camp director, he was not someone most viewers and other contestants saw as a competitor who would reach the finals, let alone win the entire competition. Plus, Dustin is a 99 percent self-taught shooter. "Dustin may be the best shooter we ever had," said Colby Donaldson. "He surprised everybody. It was across the board." Dustin is director of Camp His Way, a summer Christian kids camp and year-round retreat facility. He and his wife are also foster parents and have three children of their own.

Did you learn a lot from the experts who were on the show?

The time with the experts is very limited. You see most all of it on the show. I did pick up a few things that I brought back and will train myself with, but that limited time doesn't yield much in a competition—you pretty much just return to your prior training.

What did you learn from the other contestants?

I picked up a good bit from the other guys in the house. Sometimes all you could do was sit around and talk about guns and shooting. I remember Chris was a firearms instructor, and Paul was an MMA [mixed martial arts] fighter—so it was cool getting free lessons from these guys.

How was it living with all the other contestants? What was the best part of that? Did you form friendships or bonds with other contestants? What was the most challenging part of dealing with other contestants?

Ninety percent of the guys in the house were gentlemen and great folks. I say gentlemen and not ladies because Sara and Amanda left pretty quickly, so we hardly got to know them. Of course, our season we had Jake to deal with, so he was the adversary by his own choice, and the rest of us (both Blue and Red) were longing for him to be eliminated so we could enjoy what we came there to do. Most of the guys will be lifelong friends—I compare it to summer camp. We were all there for a good amount of time with a common purpose, and we will stay in touch for years to come.

What was the most difficult part of being on the show?

The downtime. You don't shoot nearly as much as you wish. It's so boring and unproductive in those times. And being away from your family is tough too. After halfway through, I was ready to head into any elimination so I could see my family sooner than later.

What was the most rewarding part of being on the show?

Winning. Getting to have that record of what you did on DVD is a pretty cool souvenir.

What are your favorite guns to shoot? Did you discover a type of weapon or marksmanship through this show that you really enjoyed?

The LaRue OBR was a favorite. I love the .308. That rifle is just awesome. Then the Volquartsen I-Fluted was next. Any .22 you can cut Q-tips with and hit golf balls at a hundred yards is pretty sweet.

What are you currently doing, and what is your latest activity with marksmanship?

I have folks wanting me to shoot competitively, but I have plenty of other things occupying my time. I want to teach youth fun and safe marksmanship at my camp in the off-season, so hopefully I can do that soon enough.

What are your plans for the near future?

Lots of appearances, and again the youth marksmanship camps. But I'd like to use the money to buy my family a house near the camp and continue in the camp's ministry as well as our foster care.

How did your life change from being on the show? How did you grow?

God is using my story to reach others and encourage them to live for Him, so that is the coolest thing.

Can you give any advice to marksmen who want to develop their skills? What do you recommend?

Training—not just shooting, but training and trigger control.

Are there any overall tips you can give about shooting that could help readers who are trying to improve their marksmanship?

Proper technique, and enjoy it. It's no fun if it gets to be a job. That's what gave me the best edge in *Top Shot*—I just had fun with it.

BARRETT 82A1 .50

COUNTRY: USA

CALIBER: .50 BMG (Browning Machine Gun) cartridge and 12.7x99mm NATO; also .416 Barrett

WEIGHT: 30.9 pounds for the 29-inch barrel; 29.7 pounds for the 20-inch barrel

BARREL LENGTH: 29 inches or 20 inches

FEEDING SYSTEM: 10-round detachable box magazine

ONE OF THE most amazing and memorable challenges of season two comes when marksmen test their long-distance shooting skills with the Barrett. Players have to hit a thirty-inch target at a thousand yards in the fastest time. Each competitor has a maximum of five minutes and fifteen rounds. U.S. Air Force sniper George Reinas nails the target on his first shot. But the prize in this competition goes to the one who can shoot the target the fastest—that honor goes to NRA national pistol champ Brian Zins.

Snipers use this antimatériel Special Application Scoped Rifle to take out targets at superlong distances with surgical precision. Soldiers can disable radar cabins, trucks, and parked aircraft with the weapon. It was used in operations Desert Shield and Desert Storm in Iraq. The bullet travels faster than the speed of sound, so marksmen see the impact before they hear it.

Designed in 1980 by Barrett Firearms Manufacturing, the first and only .50-caliber semiautomatic rifle takes a ten-round magazine and offers low perceived recoil and self-loading action. Such a powerful weapon comes with a powerful price of about $8,900. The rifle has a long effective range of 1.1 miles. Typically shot supported by a bipod. For a big gun, the recoil is strong (like an aggressive shoulder push), but not as powerful as a 12-gauge shotgun held to the shoulder, because the recoil system cushions the blow.

VLTOR TS3 CARBINE

COUNTRY: USA

CALIBER: 5.56 NATO

WEIGHT: 7 pounds, 7 ounces

BARREL LENGTH: 15 inches

IN SEPTEMBER 2011, *Top Shot* introduced the TS3 carbine as a high-tech evolution of the military's M4 carbine. On season three, competitors had to run an elaborate relay race based on Special Weapons and Tactics (SWAT) training. Teams shot targets from seventy-five to a hundred yards from five elevated platforms, competing in a relay, using the Vltor TS3 carbine. Colby calls the gun "so cutting-edge that *Top Shot* has received the first production models ever made." Season one winner Iain Harrison returns to the show, along with season two winner Chris Reed, to lead the teams.

The rigid polylithic upper receiver offers remarkable stability, strength, and optics mounting solutions; the improved buffer and recoil system further add to the weapon's reliability, while reducing recoil and making the weapon more controllable. Finally, the exclusive enhancements of the Vltor lower receiver and stock assembly make what was one of the most ergonomic platforms in history even more comfortable and practical to shoot.

SPANISH-AMERICAN WAR 1898 3.2-INCH BAG GUN

COUNTRY: AUSTRIA

WEIGHT: 1,390 pounds

FEEDING SYSTEM: Individual 14-pound shrapnel shells

CONTESTANTS COMPETE IN the elimination challenge using the biggest gun of the series so far—the Spanish-American War 1898 3.2-inch bag gun. Hitting the targets requires the shooters to adjust the cannon to line up accurately and hit targets with aluminum projectiles. The rare Skoda Austrian mountain cannon is also referred to as a "bag gun," because it too fired cannonballs using individual bags of powder. The gun was developed through the Austro-Hungarian army's

efforts to create a mountain gun that could be broken down fast and easily carried by mules. The cannon can hit targets at ranges up to 7,655 yards. This weapon was known as the workhorse of the Spanish-American War. Today a functioning specimen can sell for more than $100,000.

MK32A1 GRENADE LAUNCHER

COUNTRY: USA

CALIBER: 40 mm (40x50mm)
WEIGHT: 72.5 pounds
BARREL LENGTH: 16.25 inches
FEEDING SYSTEM: Belt

IN THE ELIMINATION challenge of season four, episode four, shooters compete to hit a series of targets using a grenade launcher. On "go," each shooter starts loading grenades into his launcher and sending them out toward their respective targets. The contestant who explodes all targets first wins. Introduced into U.S. military service in the late 1960s, the MK launcher has been used in the Vietnam War, Operation Iraqi Freedom, and the Gulf War, and it is still in use today.

Manufactured by Saco Defense Industries (now a division of General Dynamics Armament and Technical Products), the grenade launcher is so effective that it can blast through infantry fighting vehicles and armored personnel carriers.

An expensive piece of equipment, at about $20,000 per unit, the belt-fed launcher fires off 40mm grenades at a practical rate of sixty rounds per minute (rapid) and forty rounds per minute (sustained). Operating on the blowback system, chamber pressure from each fired round loads and recocks the launcher. Grenades can reach a maximum distance of about 2,212 yards, with an effective distance of 1,500 yards. The main ammunition for the MK 19 model launcher is the highly explosive M430 grenade, which can kill anyone within the radius of just over five yards, and wound at about sixteen yards. The MK features a flash suppressor to protect the eyesight of the shooter.

William Bethards
Fredericksburg, Virginia
Former Marine / FBI Law Enforcement
Specialist
Age: 47

WILLIAM BETHARDS HAS done so much in his life that it's hard to keep track. A former marine and ex–Virginia state trooper with national and state three-gun championships under his belt, he now serves as a firearms instructor for the FBI. This smiling sharpshooter also works as a real estate agent, is a deacon in his church, and rebuilds classic Corvettes on the side. William spent eleven years on the Marine Corps Shooting Team, where he also coached for a while. In 1994 he won the coveted Lauchheimer Trophy (Gold), awarded each year to the top rifle and pistol shooter in the entire corps. He is currently the FBI shooting team national record holder in three-gun. To top it all off, he also shoots Olympic-style compound bows—but he does it just for fun in what little spare time he has.

How did you find the experience of being on the show?

It's a unique situation that we're in. You could say it's a very blessed one. We really get to go to *Top Shot* and compete in all these different events. I truly like to say it is Disneyland for shooters, for someone with my background, having been in the military for twenty-plus years and in the shooting world a really long time. I was an artillery guy—you get to see and do a lot of things and fire a lot of weapons, but not in the arena or the same situation where you're having fun. It's kind of like playing with boy toys.

In layman's terms, I enjoyed every single one of the challenges.

It left you with your mouth drooling, and hanging on the edge of your seat wanting more, whether you were just going to a practice or were in an elimination or going through a challenge with the other teams. With most of us and these weapons, we maybe had seen them in a magazine, but we'd never had a chance to fire them. For me, being able to get behind some of the newer weapons that have just come on the market, or the first something, like a Webley lever-action gun—I had never fired one of those before. I know someone who has one, but it's a box gun; it's a shelf gun. It's worth $18,000 or $19,000—you can barely get close to it.

We fired the Kentucky flintlock pistol, and I really liked that gun, because, being a gun guy . . . it would be the equivalent of being a carpenter, and instead of having a Sears Craftsman power tool, you have to use a saw. That's why I loved that gun so much. There's a lot involved in shooting that gun. There are so many intricate details about loading that gun, from loading the bullet down the barrel, to priming it, to pouring the powder in the flint tray, and cocking it and making sure the striker and things of that nature are in place. And then when you fire that thing, since the powder has to burn, there is a long, exaggerated follow-through or delay that the gun has that increases your follow-through or exaggerates your follow-through—you have to have one, and then the gun goes bang.

I'm a gun guy. It doesn't matter what it is. If it has sights and a trigger, I can shoot it. Anytime we were firing handguns, I knew I could put the needle on the record with that thing, regardless of what it was. I know how to align the sights, press the trigger, and stand still, and that's what I'm known for. If you have the basics of any firearm down, that's all that's required. Handguns are really my forte, so I enjoyed shooting any of the semiautomatics—all of the revolvers, especially the .22 caliber weapons, be it rifles or pistols. I really enjoyed shooting them.

I was waiting for knife throwing, ax throwing, rock throwing, or boomerang, but we didn't see any of those things early on, so I think I had an advantage going into the competition early on, because there were a lot of handguns.

If I could do it all over again, I'd probably volunteer for a lot more eliminations. That's because of the weapons they got to shoot. That was the high-speed, low-drag stuff. Not only that, but you get a little bit of TV time when you go to eliminations.

It's kind of hindsight, but they got to shoot a lot of the cool stuff. Every time someone went to elimination there was something blowing up, and whenever you can combine actual pistol or rifle shooting with something blowing up, that's a good time right there.

I liked the big bag gun. The better part of my Marine Corps career was as an artilleryman. A lot of things were the same—they were just basically updated a little bit—the sights and the way you put the sights on the gun, and the way you had to lay the gun and make sure that things were level and make sure that the traverse and elevation were similar. Things are easier to move because of gearings or bearings in more modern-day artillery, but I was absolutely amazed that they had that type of foresight and technology back in that day, because I had never fired one [of those firearms]. You see that stuff in museums. You don't get to shoot them. As a matter of fact, most of it is demilitarized so you can't shoot it. It was a dream come true, really, to say I fired that thing. It would rattle the fillings in your teeth.

I was amazed at how accurate it was, and we were pretty crappy at it. The expert, from what I understand, put three rounds right on top of one another in the center of that thing within a couple of minutes, and he did it all by himself, and he was doing it all by himself as quickly as we were, and he was deadly accurate.

I think one of the things that intrigues me the most about *Top Shot* is who comes up with these ideas of how you're going to shoot this thing. The one thing I could count on was that after the practice, you were going to be using that gun, but you could almost count on the fact that either you were going to be moving, the target was going to be moving, or both. It wasn't going to be a normal platform that you were going to be firing the weapon from.

Tell me about life around the house—how was that?

I was the grill master. Guys would come and get me out of bed and have me cook a steak for them. They wanted it done right, and I enjoyed doing it. I would rest in the afternoons sometimes to beat the heat. It would be 105 degrees some days. And you'd go lie back on your rack until the sun went down and wait for night. And that's when we all liked to go outside just to look at stars and see how many satellites we could see go by, because the sky was so clear. We didn't have TV, radio, no books, no communication. Right toward the end, they gave us a book. Most of us spent most of the time writing in our diaries. That was our release—documenting everything that we had done that day. We all enjoyed that. We really did. We all kept really good diaries. Some of these were play by play. Some were writing every five minutes.

We cooked a lot, and made our own recipes. We played a lot of cards. Some played chess or checkers, but most of the time we played a lot of cards. We made weapons. They brought us tools at one point. We were making our own blow-guns and atlatls. We were holding competitions inside the house and destroying it, shooting at the paintings with the blow-dart gun because it was the only target we had. They made us stop, because we were destroying the house, and they had to return all the stuff to IKEA or something like that. Dylan and Gary Shank made an atlatl that actually worked.

They carved one up with some really tough wood or bamboo shoot we found around that house. Cannibalized some decorations around the house. With the blowguns, we were actually hunting rabbits with them. We killed a couple rattlesnakes with the blowguns. They were very accurate and very good. We used clothes hangers and sharpened them on the stones at the house. We made some slingshots.

We worked out a lot too—myself, Kyle, Iggie, and even Gabby and Terry. We were challenging one another with the workouts. I'm really good at throwing horseshoes as well. I'm just as competitive at horseshoes as I am at shooting. I think I could make a living out of it, actually.

What's life like after the show?

Since I've been on *Top Shot*, I've dusted my guns off, pulled them out of the mothballs. Juices are flowing again. I'd like to get into the competitive spirit again and really get my guns shooting. On the competitive side, I've linked up with Brian Zins and Cabot Guns, and they're going to be sponsoring me to shoot for them. They are an awesome handgun manufacturer. We've put together a Bullseye team, and we're going to be competing internationally. I've linked up with a good friend of mine who was on the Marine Corps International Shooting Team—Richard Grey—and I'm tuning up with him. I'm going to go down to Benning and try to make the U.S. team, and hopefully make the Olympic team shooting free pistol and air pistol. I've shot competitively before. I was a competitive shooter while I was in the Marine Corps, and I shot both on the conventional and international shooting teams. I'm a little older and wiser now, and I probably can pull it out. I'm settling in. The older you get, the better you get. Your heart rate gets lower—your concentration level is more intense. A lot of things don't go in and out of your head. When I was young, I was worrying about my daughter, or my wife would tell me to pick something up at the store. I would think about things I needed to do—cutting the grass. As you become more accomplished in your life, you're able to focus more intently on one thing, and that's what you want to do. When you're competing, you have to put the needle on the record every single time.

MOSSBERG 500 CHAINSAW SHOTGUN, FS 2000

COUNTRY: USA

CALIBER: 12-gauge, 20-gauge, .410-bore

WEIGHT: 5.75 pounds

BARREL LENGTH: 18.5 inches

FEEDING SYSTEM: 5-round capacity, internal tube

INTRODUCED AT SHOT Show 2011 by O. F. Mossberg, this shotgun is a pistol-grip, pump-action shotgun with no stock. Its build is based on the Mossberg 500 shotgun, which employs hammerless pump-action repeaters. The gun is suitable for home protection but is difficult to control. The Mossberg shotguns appear in many action movies, including *Zombieland*. Many shooters think this weapon may be the perfect zombie killer. In season four, shooters must enter three different rooms one at a time by breaching them with the shotgun. Once the door is breached, competitors enter an alleyway and make their way to multiple targets. They repeat this three times, and the fastest wins.

The "chain saw" of the name comes from its wraparound chain saw–style handgrip. The gun is designed to be shot from the hip. Shooters grab hold of a top handle to guide and maneuver the gun. The shotgun has a door-breaching muzzle, and three rails allow for the mounting of accessories.

SLINGS

AND

ARROWS

WHILE *TOP SHOT* mostly challenges competitors with firearms, the show puts marksmen to the test on all levels—including using weapons that have nothing to do with explosions. Many of these weapons go back to early times, including knives, bows and arrows, hatchets, blowguns, and even stones. A true marksman has to know how to hit the bull's-eye with not just pistols and rifles, but with all weapons. While some of the top shooters sailed through challenges with a squeeze of the trigger, the more primitive weapons often posed difficulties. Some players were surprised to find how hard hurling a knife or hatchet on target was compared to hurtling lead downrange. While season three winner Dustin Ellermann smoked most challenges, he fell to Cliff Walsh when it came to knocking off tin cans with stones, by a score of five to one. When it came to tossing knives, many players faced the clang of defeat as they failed to throw with the proper fluidity and technique that would make a knife stick. About throwing the bowie knife, Peter Palmer said, "When it sticks, it seems really awesome. It's like, *foonk*. It's like redeeming. You say, 'Yeah, that's right!' But when you miss, it's like, *poowang*—'You failed!' It's taunting you with the noise. It's really bad." Season two's tomahawk challenges also took some marksmen off guard, as they had to toss the bladed instrument just so to nail the target. George Reinas, the highly skilled military sniper who loves shooting big guns, said, "Out of everything we've shot here, if you told me the tomahawk was going to be the most intense thing you do, I'd be like, 'Yeah, dude . . . whatever, bro.' But it was."

The bow and arrow is probably one of the most common nongun weapons that has appeared throughout *Top Shot*. To this date, archery remains one of the most popular tests of a true marksman. Archery is an Olympic sport, with individual and team competitions. The use of the bow and arrow as a weapon dates to earliest human history. The earliest evidence of bows and arrows goes back to the time of the cavemen in the Paleolithic era, 10,000 to 9,000 B.C. Depictions of the weapon are found throughout ancient civilizations, including among the Egyptians, Greeks, and Chinese. In ancient Greek mythology, Artemis (or Diana in Roman mythology) was the huntress, and often depicted carrying a bow and arrow. The bow and arrow was truly a weapon that spanned a wide range of cultures, from fourteenth-century England with tales of Robin Hood to primitive indigenous peoples—the Pirahã people of the Amazon and Native American Indians. While traditional bows and arrows are still in use, innovation has led to the compound bow, which uses a levering system of a pulley and cables to bend back very stiff limbs to provide more power for the archer. Some bows are even fitted with modern-day scopes for aiming. As firearms developed, the popularity of weapons like the bow and arrow declined. But throughout the 1900s and into the twenty-first century, interest in the weapon has grown as a form of competition, and for recreational sport and hunting.

Unlike with shooting a firearm, archery and knife throwing can require more physicality, motion, and strength. The pull of the bow and the strength required to hold it up certainly tired out Maggie Reese in season two and led to her elimination. Just as with firing a gun, stance is critical. How an archer places his or her feet and distributes his or her weight can make a difference in the course the arrow takes as it zings through the air. As with guns, grip is a factor as well. The wrong grip (on both the bow and the arrow) can cause an arrow to twist and turn and soar off target. Learning to aim is another basic essential for any type of marksman. Archers need an anchor point on the face where the string is pulled at full draw, and follow-through helps maintain a steady shot—moving your head or dropping your arm will lead to a miss. And just as with firearms, breathing and relaxing only add to accuracy.

As Colby Donaldson says, becoming a Top Shot means that you are a good marksman not just with one weapon, but with every weapon, and the challenges involving archery, knife throwing, and more primitive weapons have certainly put competitors to the test.

LONGBOW

COUNTRY: ENGLAND

HEIGHT: 4 to 6 feet

WEIGHT: About 1 pound

PROJECTILE: Arrows

USING A FIBERGLASS version of the English longbow, marksmen in the season one episode titled "Archer Enemies" shoot at a thirty-foot target from one hundred yards, and the contestant who lands the arrow closest to the bull's-eye wins the challenge. Longbow arrows can travel up 150 miles per hour. In the Middle Ages, the weapon was so important that all Englishmen were required by law to train with it, and the typical English archer could shoot up to fifteen arrows a minute at his enemy. Sometimes called the Welsh longbow, this weapon is traditionally made of yew (sometimes ash or elm) and is about four feet to six feet tall, and was used for everything from hunting to medieval warfare. In ancient times, strings were made of hemp, flax, or silk. Common arrows of the time were the steel broadhead, designed to deliver a wide cutting edge that could kill quickly, and the iron bodkin, made to pierce armor. Most modern arrows measure thirty to thirty-eight inches. They are often made with pine or cedar shafts, but also aluminum, carbon-fiber reinforced plastic, or other composite materials. Arrows are checked for straightness and alignment, and often coated in protective polyurethane. Feathers attached to the back of the arrow shaft make them aerodynamic and are often made of plastic today.

The modern English longbow, made of fiberglass and wood, has a forty-pound draw weight, or pullback pressure. Compare that to bows from Roman times that could have a 180- to 200-pound draw weight. Synthetic material (often Dacron) is used to make the string. Today's longbows have a useful range of up to two hundred yards.

WEAPON TALK

Fletching

The feathers on an arrow.

WEAPON TALK

Riser

The center of the bow.

RECURVE BOW

COUNTRY: USA

POUNDAGE (the amount of weight required to draw the bowstring to 28 inches, which is the standard draw length): Most bows used for target shooting have a weight of at least 25 pounds.

LENGTH: 48 inches to 66 inches is a standard size.

WEIGHT: A 62-inch bow can weigh as little as 1 pound, 2 ounces.

EPISODE EIGHT OF season three was dedicated to the recurve bow in both the team and elimination challenges. The team challenge was especially interesting, as marksmen had to skip arrows off a ramp and then into targets mounted on rotating wheels at fifty feet. Colby describes the weapon as follows: "The recurve bow is one of the oldest archery weapons, documented as far back as the second millennium B.C. It gets its name from the outward curves at the very ends of the bow. This ancient innovation gives the recurve the capacity to store more energy than straight-limbed bows." Because the bow gives more power to the arrow compared to a straight bow, archers could carry shorter bows, making it easier to traverse through the forest or ride on horseback with the weapon. Ancient civilizations, including the Greeks, Romans, Turks, and Chinese, all used the recurve bow. The Mongols and Huns were feared for their use of the weapon, because they could fire it from horseback. Many North American bows were recurves. Today, archers still shoot the recurve for sport, hunting, and competition. Archery competitions in the Olympics feature the recurve.

The recurve is distinguished by having the tops of its limbs curving away from the shooter. Modern recurve limbs are usually made of multiple layers of fiberglass, carbon, or wood (or a combination of these) on a core of carbon foam or wood. The riser is generally a separate section in the middle of the bow, and most of today's recurves are takedown bows, meaning the limbs can be taken out of the riser for easy transport and storage.

WEAPON TALK

Draw Weight

In archery, draw weight is the effort in pounds needed to draw an arrow to a specified amount. Bows are graded according to their draw weight.

WEAPON TALK

Spine

The stiffness of the arrow shaft. An arrow with very little bend is said to have more spine.

Dylan Fletcher

Age: 30
Knife Maker
Alpharetta, Georgia

AFTER WORKING AS a graphic designer at an IT firm for five years and then at a motorcycle shop for another five, Dylan was ready to be his own boss. In 2010 he opened a custom knife-making business, Fletcher Knives. It's no surprise, then, that

Dylan considers himself pretty skilled at throwing knives; he also feels comfortable with most pistols and rifles, particularly old battle rifles and anything with iron sights.

When did you start shooting?

Gun usage and safety are real big in my family. As soon as we'll be able to talk we're learning to use a gun and carry a knife and stuff like that. When it comes time to start doing that on your own, you're good and safe with it, and know what you're doing. I was probably around three years old when I started shooting guns. My father used to tell people how, when he would take me out shooting, I wasn't high enough to see over the shooting bench, so he would pick me up and I would shoot on the bench sitting Indian style.

The first pistol I shot was an old Smith & Wesson semiauto pistol. Shortly after that my father got me a Ruger 10/22 rifle. It went from there.

My mother's side of the family is real big into archery. My grandfather on her side has hunted big, dangerous game with a bow. He, my grandmother, and my mom all did archery competitions. They were really, really good. They were kind of famous in their hometown of Memphis for doing all that stuff. They were in the newspapers all the time and everything.

I had a lot of marksmanship coming from both sides. My father was an expert—or some kind of beyond expert—in the army reserves. He was a big-time shooter.

I throw knives, but I do it for fun. I've done it since I was a kid, so I've gotten good at it. I've been carrying a knife since I was a tiny kid, and you can't carry a knife that long without throwing it at trees or up in the air and down at the ground and stuff like that.

The knives that I make . . . well, there're really two types of knives in the knife world: There are users and collector knives. The collector knives aren't meant to cut anything; they are meant to look pretty, and they are made out of real expensive materials and stuff like that. And then you've got the user side of custom knives, which are knives that are meant to perform.

They are less expensive, but they are for people who buy a knife to use, and that's the stuff that I make. I make knives for outdoor enthusiasts, military, law enforcement guys, stuff like that. I don't attack the collector market at all.

How did you get on the show?

I talked to a couple people on the show, and they said the exact same thing I did. I was watching season two, and at the very end of the season, in the "Behind the Bullet" episode, Chris Reed is sitting there and he says, basically, "I filled out the application on a whim, and so if you think that you might be able to do it, fill out the application. You never know." So I thought, *What the hell. I'll never hear anything about this, but I might as well fill the thing out. What's the worst that's going to happen?* So I walked over to my computer and filled it out, and the next thing I know, I started getting phone calls. Every single time I heard from the production company, I thought, *This is the last time I'm going to hear anything; I'd better not get excited.* And then before I knew it, I was on the show.

You keep in mind the type of people you're shooting against right off the bat. You've just gotten there and nothing's really real yet. You're just going like a zombie, getting scooted around everywhere by production people, and then all of the sudden they say, "You've got to shoot against all these people," and then you find out who everyone else is. You have world champions of this and that, and you start thinking, *Wow, there are some real good people here, and I've got to beat them just to get into the house.*

I had never done a competition other than little bitty stuff. I have a ton of friends who are expert shooters. A lot have military backgrounds—they've done sniper stuff. We've had little competitions against one another for who was going to buy the beer that day. I've never gone out and done USPSA or any of that. All I knew was that I could outshoot all my buddies, so I probably had a shot at this.

When we were in the audition process . . . you don't know anybody when you're there. I might have seen some [of them] on TV. It was clear when I was there for auditions that they might be going in a new direction. I was one of three guys who had tattoos and crazy hair.

I was just trying to have a good time. Even when times are going hard or you have differences with somebody, you're getting to do something really cool, so you might as well just make the best of everything you've got out there. I just tried to stay happy and keep myself entertained and keep everyone else entertained. Just hang around and be nice to everybody.

What were some of the challenges you liked most?

Some of the challenges I liked the most were some I didn't think I'd like the most—like when we did the flintlock pistol. I'm kind of a historical weapons expert. I know everything about every old gun ever made, and every old knife and sword ever made. So they pulled that thing out, and I had shot black-powder pistols before but never a Kentucky flintlock pistol, and none of them had ever excited me. They brought this thing out and I thought, *Oh, great—we're going to have to shoot this thing—what a waste of time.* Then we started shooting it, and it was fun loading the thing and shooting it right on the spot. The way they laid the challenge out was a ton of fun. I'm actually scared of heights—even small heights like we were standing on. I didn't like that at all. But all that together— your blood is pumping and stuff. I had a great time. We were swinging on that rope like a bunch of monkeys. We were jumping all over the place on that structure like it's a jungle gym. Just swinging on the rope when no one was filming was fun. We turned into a bunch of six-year-olds.

Poor Chee [Kwan]. It was like a cartoon. Every time he hit the wall, we were like, "Man he's hurt." Then he'd jump right back up. It was like watching Wile E. Coyote trying to catch the Roadrunner. We were joking around that someone should have painted a tunnel on the other side and he would have gone right through.

When [Gregory] Littlejohn got up there to shoot, he was standing there for a good two and a half, three hours (that's a

joke). None of us had to go to the bathroom when that challenge was over, because we had all gone during that challenge,
right there, standing there waiting for him to be done. My
joke was that we actually broke for lunch waiting for him to
be done and he was still standing there. We had a lot of fun
messing with him about that, but it was a mistake anyone
could have made. None of us made it, but he did.

The BAR challenge was fun. Not only do you get to shoot a
machine gun, but you're flying under barbed wire and jumping into a trench, and there are explosions and fireballs going
off. That's what made it cool. If you were just shooting a machine gun, you can do that at a shooting range. The fact that
you were doing it with explosions going off and stuff? That
made it awesome. It was killer. It was great.

What weapons did you enjoy?

I wanted more machine guns and psychotically cool stuff. I
know they had that eventually, but not while I was there. The
shotgun—if you're going to pick up a semiauto shotgun like a
tactical assault shotgun, the Benelli M4 is the coolest one
you could possibly shoot, and we got to shoot that. One of the
coolest crossbows made is the Stryker Crossbow. I fell in love
with that thing.

I own an M14. A lot of the stuff we got to shoot, I've shot
that stuff. The weapons I don't get to shoot at home I really
like—the BAR, the cannon—there's nothing cooler than when
that thing goes off. It's like a block of C4 going off right next to
you when that thing fires. The concussion coming out of that
thing—it moves the cannon back a good six feet every time
you fire it, and that's when it's braced and the brakes are on.
When you fire it, you can't be facing it, because the firing pin
can come out and smack you. If it hits you in the face, you've
got a serious problem, so you have to turn your back to it.
When it goes off, it shakes the ground you're standing on—
it'll knock the fillings out of your head.

You could get really accurate with it. I was pretty proud of
my shot on that thing. Not to mention you're shooting a

three-and-a-half or four-inch projectile. To be accurate with something like that at the distance we were going was fun.

What challenge was most challenging?

When we did the shotgun challenge, I was kind of stressed out at that point. I was having a little conflict. I wasn't in the right frame of mind. I shoot shotguns, and I should have had a perfect score on that thing. The second it started not going right for me, it just kind of added to the stress, and I wasn't having a good time at that point. A lot of it had to do with my sleep. I wasn't getting a lot of sleep, ever. I'm the kind of person who stays up until three o'clock in the morning every single night and gets up and goes to work at nine. Everybody was waking up at five something in the house. And it was really hot. The air conditioner didn't work in our room. I sleep in an icebox. I need to be able to hang meat in my room.

In the end, you get stuck in this house with sixteen other people, and it's not like you can relate that to anyone else who hasn't done it. It's like when people get shipwrecked on an island together; no one else is going to understand what you've been through except these people. Everyone watches this on TV and they're like, "That's not hard; that's easy." I was one of those couch commandos who was like, "I can out-shoot any of these dummies. I don't know what they're talking about with all the stress." But when you're locked in a house for a month and you're away from your family and you have to deal with all this stuff from the second you get up to the second you go to sleep, there're only a few people who understand what that's like, and it's the other people in the house with you. Even if you weren't best friends, they're the only people you can relate to about it. So you can't help but be friends with these people, and any kind of differences that you have, you still have something that bonds you together. You tend to get over conflict pretty easily with them.

When we got in the house—Blue Team and Red Team—we just looked at one another as other people in the house. We had dinner every night together that we could. And if one team was busy at elimination, the other team was busy cooking for them, so they had dinner waiting for them.

All the stuff you see us eat and cook, we made ourselves.

Do you have advice for marksmen wanting to get into this?

Luckily, we're in a generation where you can get information on anything you want. For anyone wanting to get into shooting stuff, it doesn't matter how young you are. I'm all about the youth getting involved, because if they don't like shooting, then the sport is going to die out. You have to have younger people getting into it. It's really easy if you want to get involved in competition shooting. That stuff is everywhere. You've just got to get out and find it. You have to get out to gun ranges or whatever is around. You don't have to be great. You just have to go do it.

I'm getting into shooting competitions now. It's a bunch of fun, and you get to meet really nice people. When everyone has a gun, everyone is polite. Those are the best personalities in the world.

I want to get younger people involved with it. The demographic that is out there now are military and law enforcement and more mature shooters. Not necessarily kids. I want to get people in there—everything from hunters to those who skateboard all the time. I don't think you have to be a military guy or a hunter or an older shooter—anyone can get into it and do competitive shooting. I want the demographic to change so it looks like a day at the mall and you have got everybody there.

One of the things I want to do with my *Top Shot* fifteen minutes of fame is to get the word out there that everyone can do this. I am getting into competitive shooting, and I want to drag everyone into it. I want the younger community to see I'm a regular dude—I'm just like you—I've got a skateboard and a motorcycle, and shooting is what I like. I want to show them that you can be a crazy kid with tattoos and earrings and shoot with the big dogs.

I'm talking to some firearms manufacturers right now,

and that's what I'm talking about—I want to change what the competitive shooter looks like. I want it to be the younger dude—the regular guy. And a lot of them are going after that and think it's a good idea, because obviously the more people you can pull into it, the better.

They are looking to get new blood and new looks. It will help the sport—the bigger it will get.

I want to go out and get into teaching shooting and help the youth community—right now, maybe Boy Scout and Cub Scout troops.

Right now I'm just learning the rules for competitions. I don't really know much about it. I'm getting my competition guns ready. I've gone out to talk to the local guys in my IPSC community and gotten involved with them. I'm really just getting started.

Do you have any tips?

Safety and practice. Know the weapons, and know how to operate them safely. Get all your fundamentals down and practice as much as you can. It's not like painting, where only a few people in the world are going to be great at it. With practice [at shooting], you're going to get better and better. If you're looking to get into competition shooting, that's the way. It becomes instinctual. Practice all the time.

There are a lot of aspects—you have to have your reloads down. You've got to be able to clear a malfunction. You can practice reloading your magazine right there in your living room. They make these things called snap caps, except they don't fire, and you can practice clearing jams and stuff all day long with those things. Accuracy is only half of it. You need to get everything else down.

There's an old saying: "Slow is smooth, and smooth is fast, and you can't shoot faster than you can aim." You've got to figure out at what speed you can get your weapon on target and execute your shot, and do your reloads, because if you do things correctly and it's slightly slower, it will be faster than if you go superfast and don't hit anything, or have a malfunction. It takes you longer to reload and shoot again instead of just getting it right the first time.

You actually have to plan out before you start shooting what you're going to do when your mag changes, so your gun never runs out of ammo. You don't ever want your gun's slide to walk to the rear. You want to shoot until you've still got a couple rounds in your magazine when you drop it and load the next one, so you don't have to cycle your slide forward. You're planning out before you run your challenge when you're going to do your magazine reload—you're practicing doing it. When you get up there, you have to be fast on the reloads.

Did you learn from others in the house?

One of the people who amazed me at how fast reloads can go was Gabby. That girl, when she shoots, she is the Terminator. I've never seen mag changes that fast. We would be back at the house and I would ask her questions: "How do you do that? What are you looking at?" She would tell me the strangest thing about the exact angle you're turning the handgun at in front of your face but still holding it in line with the target, and the inertia of this and that. As far as anyone in the house, she amazed me as a shooter.

Nock

A notch at either end of the bow for holding the bowstring, or the notch at the back of the arrow that fits on the bowstring. The nock point is an attachment (e.g., a small bead) at the center of a bowstring used to help mark and maintain a consistent nocking.

COMPOUND BOW

COUNTRY: USA

DRAW WEIGHT: 50, 60, 70 pounds

WEIGHT: 3.8 pounds

HEIGHT: 30.625 inches when measured axle to axle (meaning from the axle of one pulley to the axle of the other pulley)

IN 1969, HOLLESS Wilbur Allen was granted a patent for his invention of the compound bow. Evolved from the standard bow, the compound bow is powered like all bows—by its limbs. The archer pulls back on the string; the limbs compress, bending toward each other; and when the shooter releases the string, the energy from the limbs snapping back to position transfers to the arrow. Using a system of cables and pulleys, the bow requires less force to pull back the string, making it much easier to hold steady and aim than a traditional bow. The compound debuted in the U.S. national archery competition in 1970, but it wasn't until 1995 that the bow was included in the World Target Archery Championship. In season two of *Top Shot,* competitors used the Bowtech Assassin compound bow, launching arrows from thirty-five feet into tubes of decreasing diameter from three to 1.5 inches.

The power of the compound bow comes from the flexible yet strong composite material from which the bow is constructed. The compound bow is distinguished by eccentric wheels, or cams, on the upper and lower limbs. The handgrip, the arrow rest, and the sights are all incorporated in the riser. Arrows for the compound are usually aluminum alloy or carbon composite material as opposed to wood, because the bow imparts greater force on the arrows.

Kisser

The button or nodule attached to the bowstring at the nock point. Archers touch the kisser to the same spot on the face each time (sometimes the lips, hence the name).

Chris Brackett—Compound Bow Expert,

World-class Archer, and Bow Fisherman

With a bow and arrow, Brackett is able to shoot an aspirin thrown into the air from thirteen yards away.

When you say "bow," most of the time people think Robin Hood. They think of a staff that's got a piece of string on it. These compound bows have wheels, cams, pulleys, risers, and very stiff limbs that have been shortened to be able to transfer the energy with the rollover of the cam and the wheel and the spring-back of the limbs. Compound bows are the best of the best. They have at least three to four times more energy than any type of recurve or longbow. The cams on these bows [reduce] the draw weight—80 percent of the poundage that you're pulling is gone. One of the most important things to shooting any kind of bow is the forward pushing motion with one hand and the pulling back with the other. Consistency—doing the same thing over and over—pushing and pulling—that's who is going to shoot better. The sighting with a bow is really comparable to an M1 Garand rifle. The circular sight on the back of the rifle is comparable to the peep sight, which is circular. The front sight of a bow is also circular. You line those two up and now all you have to do is make sure that your aim is true and your grip is true. It's just like shooting a rifle. Form and stance are also very important. You have to address the target [position your body] as though you were going to hit a drive down a fairway toward the hole. You have to be pretty athletic to shoot a bow well.

Anchor Point

A place on the archer's face where he or she can aim from and consistently draw the bow to full length. It is the spot where the pulling hand rests on the face; it may be at the cheek or at the nose, for example.

"Straight Shooter" Challenge:
SEASON TWO

THE SETUP: Teams test their marksman skills with the Bow-tech Assassin compound bow, shooting arrows from thirty-five feet into six tubes. The arrows fly down the curved tubes, hitting a target at the end. Team members learn to aim compound bows as they would rifles, aligning front and rear sights. Chris Reed, Joe Serafini, and George Reinas have all had experience with the compound bow, and Jay Lim has a background with the recurve bow. "I bring it into the woods and destroy deer with it," said George Reinas.

THE TWIST: Tubes are in descending diameter, from three inches to 1.5 inches. Each team has to choose who will take on the targets, from easiest to hardest.

THE OUTCOME: The Blue Team is determined to win and to stay steady and focused. Ashley Spurlin advises his Blue team-mates: "Don't run like we did on the very first challenge. Keep your heart rate down." Red goes first, and the team misses several shots before they can complete the entire course. But the Blue Team gets off to a very slow start, with Ashley, Maggie, Kyle [Frasure], and Daryl each missing. Jay has the smallest tube, and although he takes his time, his arrow flies into the tube and explodes the egg at the end of the tube. But Maggie is not looking through her sights, and she continues to miss. When Colby calls time, Maggie and Darryl are left still having to hit their targets. The Blue Team is crushed. Red has now won three of four challenges. "I would say at this point right now, it's some-what of a dysfunctional family," said Ashley. "It's just total chaos right now on the Blue Team."

THE ELIMINATION CHALLENGE: The Red Team sends Maggie to elimination, because her performance had been one of the worst today and in a previous challenge. Although Kyle Frasure had performed well with the compound bow, his team feels he has had weak performance overall, and they send him to elimination. Again using the compound bow, Kyle and Maggie practice shooting from an elevated platform, as hunters do. On the day of elimination, the two shoot from a platform—twenty yards downrange are three redwood tree trunks. Behind those trunks are sixteen eight-inch targets—eight orange and eight yellow. Kyle and Maggie each have a color, and targets appear from behind the trunk for only about five seconds and then disappear. The winner is the one to hit the most targets in three minutes, or all eight targets first. Feeling weary from practice, Maggie says she's pushing every last bit of strength she has into the weapon. Kyle comes out of the gate strong, and Maggie misses with her first few arrows. But she finds her rhythm and at one point is tied four to four with Kyle. But after that she can't connect, and Kyle ends up with eight hits to Maggie's four. "I'm just proud of myself for having put myself out there and done something so weird and wild and completely out of my comfort zone," said Maggie.

BOWIE KNIFE

COUNTRY: USA

LENGTH: 12 to 30 inches

BLADE LENGTH: 6 to 24 inches

WEIGHT: 14-inch Jack Dagger bowie weighs 14 ounces

POPULARIZED BY JAMES Bowie in 1830, the bowie knife was allegedly designed by his brother Rezin and smithed by blacksmith Jesse Cleft out of an old file. (While some historians say that the famous knife maker and blacksmith James Black created that first knife, Black certainly did create the most famous version of the bowie knife in 1830 from a wooden model carved by Bowie.) James Bowie, or Jim, became famous for knives after he survived a harrowing fight in 1827 in Mississippi. Although he was stabbed with a sword and shot with a pistol, he survived, largely due to his knife. Newspapers published reports of the dramatic fight, which became known as the "Sandbar Fight," and Bowie gained notoriety for his fighting prowess and for his knife. His knife was in huge demand, and many craftsmen and manufacturers made their own versions of it. His legend caught on in England as well. British manufacturers made their own versions of the knife. It enjoyed particular popularity in the South until the Civil War, when Confederate soldiers turned to more progressive weapons with which to wage war. Many Confederate soldiers, however, carried immense knives called D-guard bowie knives, which were actually short swords often made at home from old saw or scythe blades. In the 1950s, the bowie knife witnessed a revival of sorts, as Davy Crockett and Jim Bowie were featured in books and movies. The knife also gained public appeal in the 1980s, when *Crocodile Dundee* was shown in theaters. In a memorable scene, a mugger pulls a switchblade on Dundee, who unflappably responds: "That's not a knife." Then he pulls out his bowie knife and says: "*That's* a knife." Over the

years, "bowie knife" has become a term used for any long-sheathed knife. In the "Razor's Edge" episode of *Top Shot* from season one, teams throw bowie knives at six targets from eleven feet, while balancing over a mud pit on a beam whose width decreases from one target to the next.

The bowie used on *Top Shot* was created by professional knife thrower Jack Dagger. It's fourteen inches long and weighs fourteen ounces. Designed for competitive sport throwing, the Dagger knife can be picked up and thrown by handle or blade. The blade only appears sharp—the tip is the only sharp part with this particular bowie. Many bowies that are created for hunting have a sharp blade well suited to butchering and skinning. A standard bowie knife has a blade of eight to twelve inches in length; it is 1.5 to two inches wide, with a clip-point blade and a cross guard.

EXPERT VIEW

Todd Abrams (a.k.a. Jack Dagger)— King of Fling

World Champion Speed Thrower, International Knife Throwers Hall of Fame Inductee

WHEN I WAS a kid growing up in Baton Rouge, I used to run around the backyard throwing screwdrivers into the dirt. From there I progressed to pocketknives, and I sort of terrorized the neighbors, throwing pocketknives into a fence post, skateboards, you name it. I purchased my first proper throwing knife around 1990, and I've been throwing bowie knives ever since. The bowie knife is as much a part of American heritage as baseball or apple pie. The good thing about throwing bowie knives is that with proper technique, it doesn't favor age, gender, or size. Just being able to stick a knife into a target is very difficult to learn. One of the best knife throwers in the world on the competitive circuit is only fourteen years old. The bowie knife is part ax, part tomahawk, part dagger, and extremely useful. The grip that I taught the teams is called the handshake grip. So just as you would reach forward to shake somebody's hand, you're going to shake the hand of the knife. Just curl your fingers around it and hold it at a forty-five-degree angle—very simple. You don't want to overgrip the knife by making a fist. Just use a relaxed handshake grip. If you grip it too tightly, it overspins. If you grip it too loosely, you can't get it to spin enough. Stance is extraordinarily important in learning the basics. It's much like a front-fighting stance in karate. Stand with your hips square and your feet about shoulder-width apart. Depending on whatever hand you're throwing the knife with, right or left, you take the opposite foot and step forward with a large step and keep your knees bent underneath you. That's the proper stance. One of the most common problems for guys when they're learning to throw knives is that they feel like they need to muscle it into the target. And that's just not true. You just employ good technique. It's almost a slow, elongated motion. When your arm is tense you cannot straighten it and follow through properly with good technique. A smooth windup leads to a relaxed delivery. Knife throwing and tomahawk throwing are all about spin control. As soon as that item leaves your hands, it's going to be spinning. You want to make sure that you're at the exact proper distance, that when it lands on the target, it's exactly in the position you want it to be.

The Bowie Knife

The bowie knife was especially popular from the 1830s through the Civil War. Colonel James Bowie, who made the knife famous after fending off attackers with it in a fight in 1827, died with his knife at the Battle of the Alamo in 1836. He was one of 188 Texans who defended the small mission against an overwhelming Mexican force. As the tale has it, Bowie was sick in bed during the final assault, but he defended himself with his pistols, a rifle, and the famous bowie knife. This skirmish is one of the most famous battles of the Texas revolution. Bowie knives were used by U.S. troops during the Mexican War ten years later. That two-year conflict between Mexico and the United States erupted after the United States officially annexed Texas, which Mexico still considered part of its territory. The bowie was a popular knife for self-defense during the California Gold Rush (1848–1855). In the Sierra Nevada in 1854, Captain Jonathan R. Davis single-handedly killed eleven outlaws with pistols and a bowie knife after his mining partners were shot down by bandits. Some American historians call it the most extraordinary feat of self-defense by an American civilian in the annals of frontier history. In 1849, the emancipationist Cassius Clay was speaking out against slavery at a gathering in Foxtown, Kentucky. Clay was attacked by the proslavery advocate Cyrus Turner. A fight broke out in the crowd, and Clay wound up stabbing and killing Turner with his bowie knife. The knife was popular with troops during the Civil War, especially among Confederate soldiers, who generally had inferior arms compared to the Union troops. It was used in the Civil War battles of Pea Ridge and Prairie Grove in Arkansas, and Wilson's Creek and Price's Raid in Missouri. Lewis Powell attempted to assassinate Secretary of State William Seward at the same time that John Wilkes Booth was attacking President Lincoln. Powell stabbed him repeatedly with a bowie knife, but Seward survived. The knife was used in many fights by congressmen, bankers, lawyers, doctors, business-men, and military officers. Until firearms really predominated at the end of the 1800s, it was a primary weapon of choice.

Clip Point

One of three common knife blade designs, these blades appear to have the forward third of the blade "clipped off."

Chris Reed
Age: 38
Franklin, Tennessee
Realtor

A **SELF-DESCRIBED** "**GOOD** ol' country boy," trained in the cotton fields of the Mississippi Delta, Chris says, "I can throw knives, shoot any kind of bow, and shoot slingshots. There are very few people who can cover the whole spectrum. I'm about as competitive as they come, and as tough as a rattlesnake." He was runner-up in *Field & Stream*'s 2009 and 2010 Total Outdoorsman Challenge, and he has won countless state and national championships in both archery and the long rifle.

How did you start shooting?

I grew up in the country down here in Mississippi. Everyone I knew shot. Uncles, grandparents, Daddy—even my grandmother shot. She was a crack-shot marksman with a .22 rifle. I was shooting .22s and BB guns. It was a family hobby. We'd all go hunting in wintertime, and in the off-season, we'd challenge one another. My uncle would set a shotgun shell up at fifty yards, and we'd try to hit it with a .22 rifle. We had this giant oak tree in my grandmother's front yard, next to a cottonwood tree. It was bigger than my truck around. It was just a huge tree. We shot that tree for years and years. It took about twenty years, but we basically shot that tree down. There were probably five hundred pounds of lead in that tree by the time it died. It was right off the highway. We'd have somebody watch out for cars.

I'm a hunter. My granddaddy and uncles, we had everything. Pistols, rifles. I was six or seven when I shot a .44 Magnum. It was huge.

We had a lot of guns around, between my granddaddy, uncle, and daddy. There were always a bunch of guns around me. So there were always guns to shoot.

It wouldn't matter what kind of gun I was using; we were always trying to shoot the best with it. I had an uncle who was one hell of a marksman. I spent so much time with him. He taught me how he did it. And I began challenging him.

I moved to a neighborhood where I couldn't shoot firearms in my yard, so I got into the bow and arrow when I was twelve and went to youth class competition. Then, at thirteen or fourteen, I was shooting in the open class competitions with adults. I got really good at it. I won many state champion-ships, local shoots, regional shoots—archery competitions all over the country. I signed a pro contract. I went to a pro archery school to qualify—there were about a hundred shoot-ers from all over the world. And from the school they took the top ten competitive shooters to go into the pro class. I was the number one–ranked rookie pro as an archer.

That's interesting—where did things go from there?

I wanted to own a sporting goods store. I went to college to be a civil engineer. I went to state university. Then I went to the Marine Corps and I got into an engineering MOS. I went to boot camp, and the first thing the drill instructor says is, "How many people here hunt and shoot?" and that kind of stuff. I ended up almost setting a rifle range record on Parris Island [South Carolina].

When I graduated boot camp, I was roped off with the spe-cial group for the honors graduates. I got married; I had a few kids, started a career. I got to where I was starting to build my sporting goods store. I bought forty acres of com-mercial property and built a 7,500-square-foot building. And then, damn, dude, I got diagnosed with a brain aneurysm. Then all bets were off, dude. It's the craziest shit that ever happened in my life. My daughter was two weeks old. My lit-tle boy was two years old. We had just sold our house, and we were getting ready to build a house. I had the rug snatched out from under me.

They had to do a craniotomy—they drilled three holes in my skull. They took a big section of my skull out; they took a piece of my face out. They went down under my brain to my ophthalmic artery. They had to put a clip on it, and clip it off to keep it from rupturing, and they deflated it—took the blood out of it. They put my head back together, screwed me all up—I got screws and shit all in my forehead. They cut all through my jaw muscles. They jacked my head up.

How do you recover from that?

It took me several years. . . . I had double vision the first couple years. I tried to shoot my bow again, and every time I looked at a dot or target, there would be two of them. I wore special glasses with prisms in them. I had them made to force my eyes to go back together—to realign. My vision was not aligned anymore, because I had lost so much blood on one side with my ophthalmic artery, which goes to your iris. I fought through that with sheer willpower and God's blessing. I finally got my vision back. I got to where I could shoot again. I started to compete a little bit. And *Field & Stream* had this deal to win $25,000 in the Total Outdoorsman Challenge. I went to my local Bass Pro Shop, and it was casting with a rod and reel, shooting with a .22 rifle, shooting a bow and arrow. There were several different events, and I thought, *Hell, I'm good with that shit anyway.* I went to the regionals. I came in second place. And I came in second place in the finals. I won the shotgun event. I won the rifle event. I won all the shooting events. I smoked them.

I had the aneurysm in 2002—and the Outdoorsman Challenge was in 2009.

I was so close to winning. I lost first place by a sixteenth of a second on my endurance time, with an endurance course. Check this out: They had a bass fishing tournament. First year I came in last place with bass fishing. The next year, in 2010, I won the bass tournament. We got to finals again in 2010; I made it to second place and it paid about $2,500.

My wife was like, "Dude, you've got to start doing something." Because this was taking up so much of my time practicing for this stuff that it was costing me money. And I'm thinking, *What the hell? I've actually done well in shotgun and rifle.* So I start looking for big shoots that pay money, and I come across the *Top Shot* deal. The Web site says $100,000— test your skill with weapons throughout history, and I'm like, *What is this shit— $100,000? Are you freakin' kidding me? That's right up my alley.*

So that's how it started?

I was a week late, missing the casting call for season one. I watched every episode of season one, and I was like, *I can do that; I can do that.* I was rocking in my seat, saying, "Why didn't I make it?" But then I saw they were casting for season two, and I went online and filled out the application. I gave them half a page of why I thought I could win, and the casting director called me back. I talked to him for thirty minutes out in the yard walking around. I was freakin' out, dude. I told my wife, "Do you know who that was? It was freakin' *Top Shot!*" I was going nuts. My casting director said, "Whatever you do, if you get another callback just tell them exactly what you told me."

We sent in videos. It was a big process, and then I got the call—"You made the house. You made it." And I was like, *Holy shit!* And then I started getting scared about being on a reality show, and thinking, *That's not me.* I remember the first season, doing all that "rat fink" shit and dogging one another out. I used to fight a lot. I was never good with arguing with people. I was always like, "Hell, dude, let's get it on." I thought I'd get kicked off for hitting somebody.

I didn't want to get upset and jump on somebody and get in trouble. Going through all I went through, though, had made me a wiser, smarter person—more civil. It calmed me down a little bit. I appreciated life. I was brought up as a Christian, and everyone would just be nice—we wouldn't need laws and everything.

Me and Jay bonded out of that deal probably as good as anybody did. He was having some problems early on. We had several conversations at two o'clock in the morning about how his team was feeling about him. I just tried to encourage him to be mindful of how he was coming across to some of these people. He wasn't meaning to be negative—he was trying to offer constructive criticism, but a lot of these guys were marine gunnery sergeants, and they didn't want his advice. "Just keep it to yourself. If they ask for it, fine. But don't be just offering that shit." He meant no ill will.

I convinced him to just apologize and work together as a team. They were just self-destructing. We wanted it to be a competition, and shoot against some good shooters. We wanted the best shooter to win the competition, and that's what our team originally agreed on. Some people got the misconception that we were trying to do some sneaky stuff and some buddy deals. But we made a pact early on that we weren't going to finagle it to weed out the good shooters. We were trying to weed out the bad shooters.

How did you pick your team—which turned out to be the winning team?

It was a lot of good instinct, intuition, and reading people. Just knowing who you can count on. I graduated from a little high school—thirty people in my senior class. We played football. This school had never won a state championship, never done anything. And we had a group of guys, and we brought back an old coach. He was a retired marine—he taught our fathers back in the day. They brought him out of retirement to coach my junior and senior years in high school. We went to state championship junior year, and we got beat. We went to state championship my senior year, and we won. So—check this out—the end of my third quarter senior year, I got hit in my left leg and broke my leg. Had five screws put in my knee. I got to watch the game, and we won. We were the pride of the school. The group of guys we had—we played, like, Ironman football, because we didn't have enough to have offense and defense. We played it all, dude. We had a bond. We were tight. We had a brotherhood. And I carried that type of experience with me—knowing how to form a team, a support system. To help one another when we're down; don't start nagging on one another. If somebody knows something to help the group, let's share it. You got something you want to say, don't hold it back. Let's get this shit out. So it worked out good. We all made the best of it. And we had a lot of veterans in there. We all had been in close quarters together.

We had all been in shit together. And that helped us a lot. We had lived like that and in worse conditions. We could make the best of it.

How did you like the big guns?

Shooting the Barrett at a thousand yards—that was a long way. There was a strong crosswind. You had to aim at one mountain in order to hit the other mountain. That gun was like an earthquake going off. There wasn't a whole lot of re-coil, just a tremendous amount of percussion. It felt like you were pulling a trigger on an earthquake.

That was a big machine.

Shooting the Benelli M2 shotgun—it was tricked out. It was a sweet-shooting shotgun. When I went to go practice with it, they gave me fifty rounds and forty clay targets, and I busted forty clay targets and I had nine rounds left. I felt like, "I got this, baby."

What was the finale like?

Once we had gotten down to the final three, we had been there so long and we were so ready to go home—we were all good with being first, second, or third—we didn't care who won it. It was just me, George [Reinas], and Gunny [Brian Zins]. We get to the final three—with my brain surgery, I have had terrible shit to deal with—I was having one of them days. I had some nervousness about me. I wasn't feeling real good. The day had dragged on. George called it out—he said, "Chris just isn't himself today." That was shit I was dealing with. Gunny gets up and makes his couple shots. He's two for two, and George finally hit one, and I have none. So Gunny and George are in, and George pulls his infamous stunt where he picks this easy-ass target and just misses it intentionally to keep me in the game and make it more of a competition be-tween me and him. Once we even the score up, we go to the next weapon—Sharps rifle—and we were lucky to hit any-thing with it. We had both shot it, and it was shooting, like, a foot and a half high and six inches to the left. We knew it was going to be a crapshoot, and luckily I hit it, and he missed. There went that. Then it was just me and Gunny left. That was a pretty emotional deal for me and George. Out of the goodness of his heart, he did that. He didn't want the competition to be over. He wanted it to be down to shot-for-shot. He did me a great favor. I kept telling him, "Dude, as good a token of friendship as that was, I was like, 'You stupid son of a bitch, I wasn't out of it yet. If you had hit the plate and I had hit the plate, I still had one more gun coming.'" I was like, "Dude, I could have shot my way out of this. You didn't have to do this." He thought it was going to be over too early. But we had, like, two more shots coming. I could have caught back up.

When I won, it was a flood of emotions. Tears came to my eyes. The first thing I do—George starts hugging the shit out of me—he's a huge monster of a man, and he's bawling like a little baby, dude, and I'm bawling. And I'm like, "Man, I can't believe this; we're doing this shit." It was the culmination of all the shit I had gone through my whole life, and for it to play out like that was an awesome reward.

I liken it to the little woodpecker pecking at a giant oak tree, like he done pecked through all of the tree, but he's not quite all the way through. But he's like, "Never give up." He looks around like, "Should I stop or should I keep going?" He's almost there. Well, I never give up.

Cross Guard

A metal bar set at right angles at the base of the blade separating the blade and the grip. Its purpose is to prevent the blade from sliding down, harming the hand or wrist of the wielder.

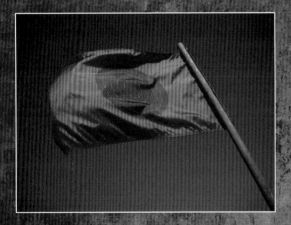

TOMAHAWK

COUNTRY: USA

LENGTH: 19.25 inches for some competitive throwing tomahawks

BLADE: 4 inches for some throwing tomahawks

WEIGHT: 1 pound, 6 ounces for some throwing tomahawks

IN SEASON TWO, teams squared off in a tomahawk-throwing contest, trying to hit an unbroken line of four targets to win in a game similar to tic-tac-toe. The tomahawk, sometimes called "the hawk," is a tool commonly associated with Native Americans. It was also used among colonial Europeans for chopping, hunting, and other work, but also for hand-to-hand fighting and as a throwing weapon. "Legend has it that when two warring tribes decided to make peace, they would literally bury a tomahawk, giving rise to the expression 'Bury the hatchet,'" says Colby Donaldson. Tomahawk throwing has grown in recent years as a sport, and it is a category in competitive knife throwing. American soldiers in Afghanistan were equipped with modern-day tomahawks to be used as tools and for combat. Resembling a hatchet with a straight shaft handle, the tomahawk originally had a stone head, but later iron and brass were used.

BLOWGUN
COUNTRY: VARIOUS

CALIBER: Darts and blowguns have caliber measurements. Common calibers are .625 and .76.

LENGTH: Modern hunting blowguns range in length from 1 foot long to 6 feet long.

WEIGHT: A .625-caliber big-bore blowgun weighs 1.2 pounds.

IN SEASON TWO, teams competed with the tomahawk, and when it came time for the elimination challenge, the theme continued as Daryl Parker and Chris Tilley went head-to-head in a blowgun contest. From thirty feet away, players had to shoot at separate grids of thirty-two balloon targets. The twist was that each balloon had another inside, and the sharpshooters could break only the outer balloon. "For this challenge, competitors needed to have a good, strong set of lungs," said Colby. "The blowgun has been used for centuries by indigenous peoples around the world to hunt small game. Today, modern blowguns are part of a growing sport using primitive weapons." The blowgun is a prehistoric weapon, and the earliest types were made of natural plant material, such as bamboo or cane. The first written references to blowguns appear in Rome in the second century, and in China between A.D. 265 and 429. A fourteenth-century French illuminated manuscript depicts a boy shooting a rabbit with a blowgun. Blowguns are used today by some hunters to kill small game; some use tranquilizer darts to capture wildlife. Professional competitions are dedicated to blowgun marksmanship, including International Fukiyado Association events and the Cherokee Annual Gathering Blowgun Competition.

Blowguns are tubes that shoot small projectiles using only the user's breath. The latest versions of blowguns are made from aluminum (sometimes carbon-reinforced plastic) and often fire four- to six-inch darts. The longer the tube, the better the accuracy and velocity. The mouthpiece is designed to provide a tight seal for the shooter to exert air pressure and hence obtain a high dart velocity. Blowgun darts can travel at a speed of four hundred feet per second. They are fast, silent, and ideal for hitting targets at short distances. Most regular blowgun users need a type of ramrod to dislodge darts that become stuck in the tube.

SLINGSHOT

COUNTRY: USA/BRITAIN

MODERN SLINGSHOT
Based on Historic Slingshot

IN SEASON ONE in the eighth episode, Denny Chapman met his elimination when he went up against Peter Palmer picking off targets with a modern-day slingshot. Standing at a distance of twenty feet, they had to nail eight-, ten-, and twelve-inch targets in sixty seconds, trying to hit only those targets with their assigned color. Slingshots developed as homemade weapons, and traditionally they rely on strong elastic material to shoot. They often use vulcanized rubber (or similar materials), which was invented by Charles Goodyear in 1839. The weapon is often associated with young troublemakers, but it can be used for small-game hunting—rabbits, quail, squirrels, and similar. By 1918, commercially made slingshots were being produced, and after World War II, they gained popularity for sport and pastime. In the 1940s, the National Slingshot Association opened in California, organizing competitions and slingshot clubs nationwide. In 1948, the Wham-O company began selling a slingshot suitable for hunting. Slingshots go by other nicknames, including "bean shooter," "flip," "shanghai," and "catapult." There has been some defensive military use of the slingshot, and in 2003 Saddam Hussein, the dictator of Iraq, released a video showing how to use the slingshot as a possible insurgency weapon.

In its simplest form, the slingshot is a Y-shaped branch with an elastic band strung across the top of the Y. The user holds the bottom of the Y as the handle, places a projectile in the center of the band, pulls back, and fires. Slingshot innovation took a leap forward in the 1950s, when the Wrist Rocket Company (later named Trumark) produced a slingshot made of bent steel rods and featuring a brace that went over the wrist and provided support on the forearm. Rubber tubing replaced the flat bands that had been in common use. A leather pad typically holds the projectile in the center of the tubing. Shooters have to be aware of possible band failure, especially at the fork end. If a band breaks at the fork end, it can snap back into the user's face and cause real injury. Modern slingshots can even come with laser sights. They can shoot at high velocity with great accuracy. Popular models include the "Black Widow" and the "Laser Hawk."

ATLATL, OR WINGER

COUNTRY: VARIOUS

LENGTH: 21 to 22 inches
WEIGHT: As little as 2 ounces

FEATURED IN SEASON four of *Top Shot*, the atlatl is another prehistoric weapon. It was used by early humans in Europe and America. It works on the same principle as many ball throwers for dogs that have plastic shafts with a tennis ball at one end. The atlatl is a shaft with a cup or spur attached. A dart or spear rests in the device, with the back end of the dart in the cup. Holding the end opposite the cup, the thrower coordinates the upper arm and wrist to fling the weapon, sending the dart through the air at speeds upward of ninety miles per hour. The people of New Guinea and the Australian aborigines still use spear-throwing devices like this. It is considered primarily a hunting weapon. Some anthropologists say the weapon had an equalizing effect among tribespeople, because to hurl it properly requires skill rather than strength. The atlatl has gained popularity in competitive sport. A few colleges have atlatl teams, including Franklin Pierce College and the University of Iowa.

While the atlatl itself is often shy of two feet long, the darts, or spears, are four feet to nine feet in length, and very thin at ⅜ to ⅝ of an inch in diameter. A finely tuned atlatl can be used to throw a dart 120 to 150 yards, with accuracy at thirty to forty yards.